Class Focus Book

Written and edited by
Sheila Ebbutt and Mike Askew

with contributions from
Len Frobisher and Janine Blinko

Place value grid

100 000	200 000	300 000	400 000	500 000
10 000	20 000	30 000	40 000	50 000
1000	2000	3000	4000	5000
100	200	300	400	500
10	20	30	40	50
1	2	3	4	5
0·1	0·2	0·3	0·4	0·5
0·01	0·02	0·03	0·04	0·05

600 000	700 000	800 000	900 000
60 000	70 000	80 000	90 000
6000	7000	8000	9000
600	700	800	900
60	70	80	90
6	7	8	9
0·6	0·7	0·8	0·9
0·06	0·07	0·08	0·09

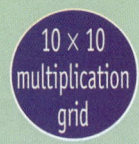

10 × 10 multiplication grid

×	1	2	3	4	5	6	7	8	9	10
1	1	2	3	4	5	6	7	8	9	10
2	2	4	6	8	10	12	14	16	18	20
3	3	6	9	12	15	18	21	24	27	30
4	4	8	12	16	20	24	28	32	36	40
5	5	10	15	20	25	30	35	40	45	50
6	6	12	18	24	30	36	42	48	54	60
7	7	14	21	28	35	42	49	56	63	70
8	8	16	24	32	40	48	56	64	72	80
9	9	18	27	36	45	54	63	72	81	90
10	10	20	30	40	50	60	70	80	90	100

1–100 grid

1	2	3	4	5	6	7	8	9	10
11	12	13	14	15	16	17	18	19	20
21	22	23	24	25	26	27	28	29	30
31	32	33	34	35	36	37	38	39	40
41	42	43	44	45	46	47	48	49	50
51	52	53	54	55	56	57	58	59	60
61	62	63	64	65	66	67	68	69	70
71	72	73	74	75	76	77	78	79	80
81	82	83	84	85	86	87	88	89	90
91	92	93	94	95	96	97	98	99	100

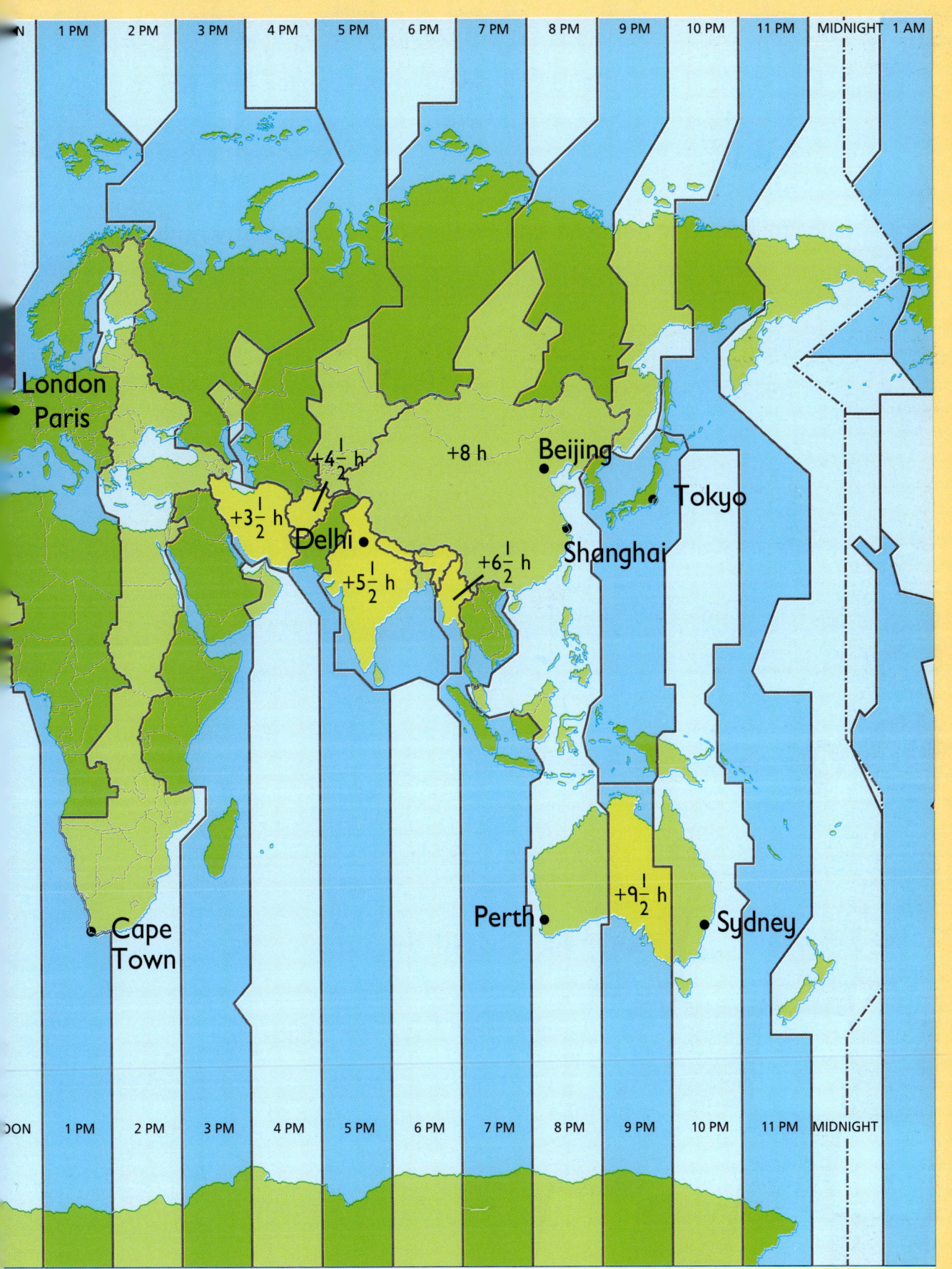

1a

1. three hundred and fifty-two thousand seven hundred and nine

2. eight million four hundred and twenty-one thousand and thirty-five

3. six million fourteen thousand nine hundred and eighty-seven

4. one million two hundred and six thousand four hundred and seventy-three

1b

A

1. 68 972 → 88 972

2. 1 357 802 → 1 397 802

3. 504 801 → 502 801

4. 8 690 042 → 8 689 042

5. 90 563 → 99 563

6. 871 279 → 869 279

B

1) 134 568 ≤ ☐ ≤ 134 598

2) 79 063 ≤ ☐ ≤ 79 072

3) 1 863 509 ≥ ☐ ≥ 1 863 489

4) 90 710 ≥ ☐ ≥ 90 699

1c

×10 ×100 ×1000

7846   9073
       1074
93·74   247·5
89·8   599

÷10   ÷100

643 889   23 572
1 934 700   21 667   6210
34 740   6832

2a

A
1. 3 × 6 × 10
2. 7 × 4 × 10
3. 8 × 9 × 10
4. 4 × 12 × 10
5. 6 × 8 × 100
6. 7 × 10 × 8

B
1. 5 × 60
2. 9 × 40
3. 80 × 7
4. 11 × 90
5. 70 × 12
6. 6 × 110
7. 7 × 900
8. 800 × 5

C

Set A	3	5	6	9	11
Set B	20	40	70	80	120

2b

A
1. 5 × 9 ÷ 10
2. 7 × 8 ÷ 10
3. 6 × 9 ÷ 10
4. 8 × 11 ÷ 10
5. 6 × 7 ÷ 100
6. 8 × 8 ÷ 100

B
1. 6 × 0·7
2. 9 × 0·3
3. 0·8 × 5
4. 12 × 0·6
5. 0·9 × 11
6. 6 × 0·03
7. 8 × 0·05
8. 0·06 × 5

C

4	× 20	× 10
5	× 3	× 100
7	× 6	÷ 10
9	× 15	÷ 100

3a
1. 2537 × 4
2. 5831 × 7
3. 6283 × 6
4. 4432 × 5
5. 3524 × 3
6. 4376 × 8

3b
1. 5·31 × 3
2. 6·23 × 4
3. 4·75 × 6
4. 7·86 × 5
5. 3·45 × 5
6. 4·27 × 7

1 An aeroplane travels 2386 kilometres between London and Athens. It makes the trip to Athens and back twice every Saturday during the summer. How far does it travel on each of those Saturdays?

2 The aeroplane uses 7 litres of fuel per kilometre. How much fuel does it use for a journey one way from London to Athens?

3 On the first flight of the first Saturday in June, the aeroplane carries 186 holidaymakers to Athens. On the second flight of the same day, the aeroplane is full with 203 passengers. How many people travel to Athens on that day?

4 Each customer pays £3.85 airport tax. Six travellers miss their flight and do not pay the tax. How much less tax gets paid on both flights in total?

5 Write a word problem using the calculation 1427 × 8, and calculate the answer.

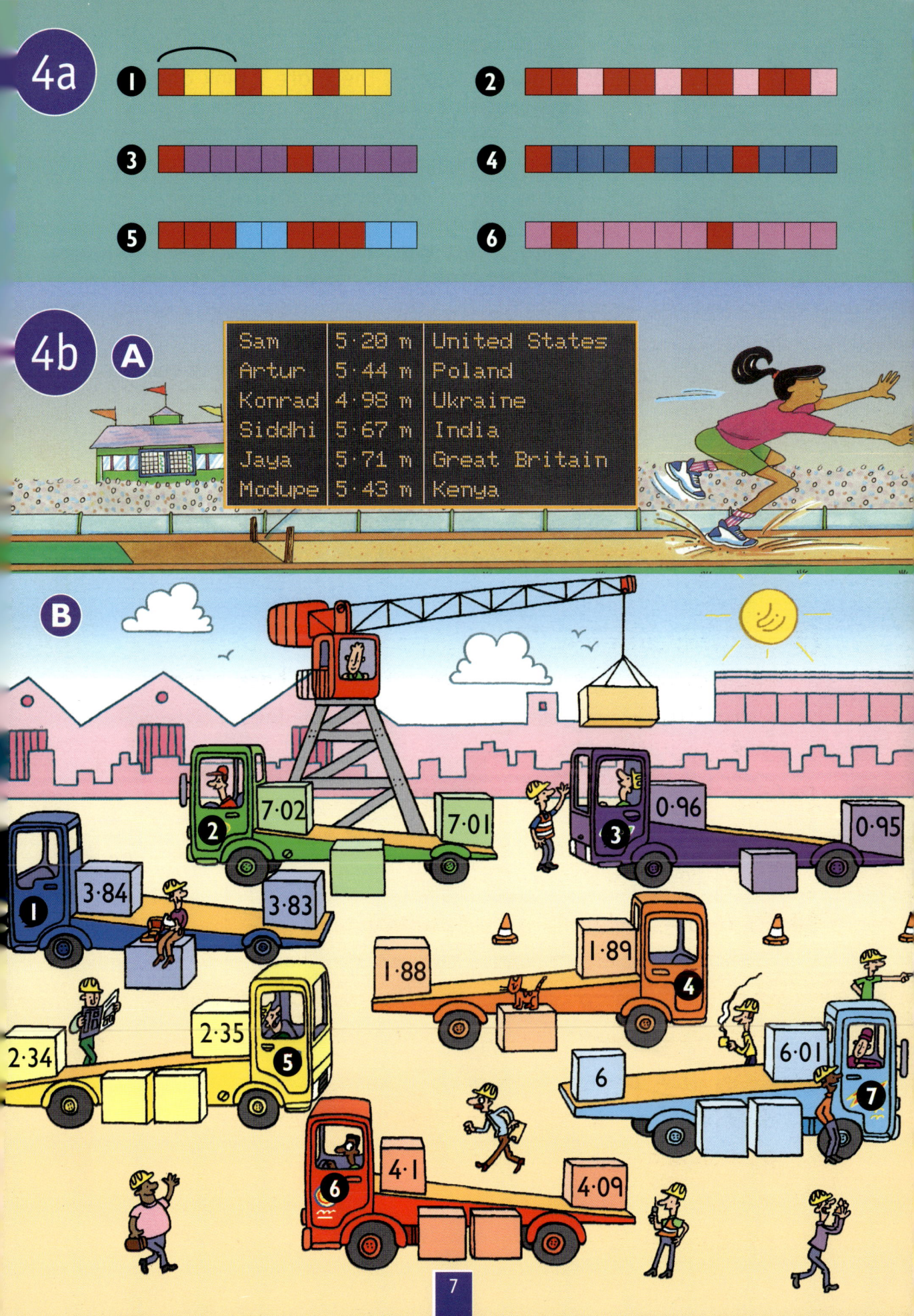

5a

1. In every box of 30 marshmallows, there are 2 pink ones for every 3 white ones. How many pink ones are in the box?

2 In a class of 30 children, 1 in 2 of the children is a girl. How many children in the class are girls?

3 On a school trip, there are 49 people altogether. For safety there is 1 adult for every 6 children. How many adults go on the trip?

4 Saroya's mum gives her 21 sweets to share with her brother. She gives him 3 sweets for every 4 she has. How many sweets does her brother get?

5 A machine making CDs produces one faulty CD in every 1000 it makes. At the end of a day it has made one million CDs. How many faulty CDs has it produced?

5b

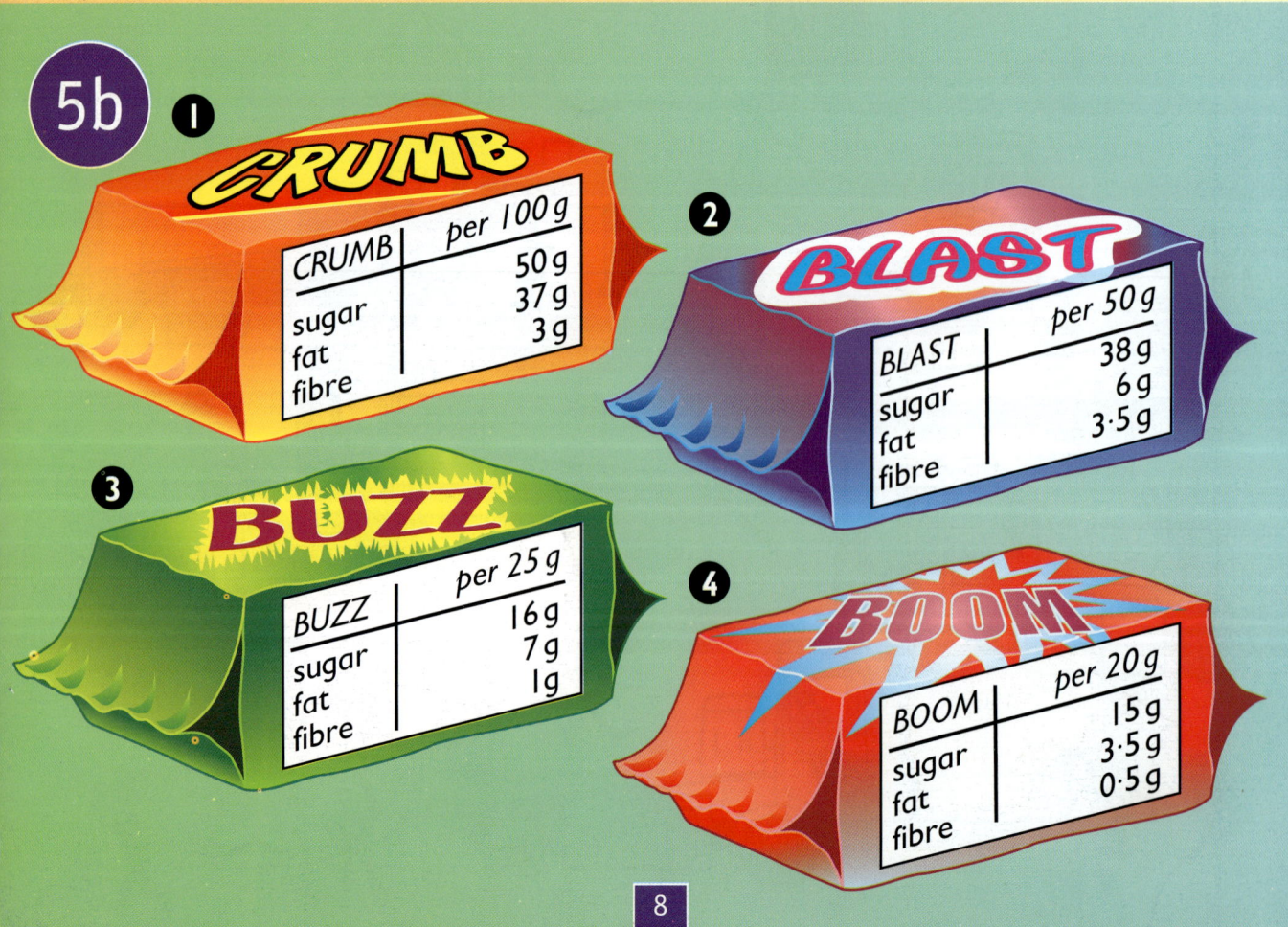

1 CRUMB — per 100 g: sugar 50 g, fat 37 g, fibre 3 g

2 BLAST — per 50 g: sugar 38 g, fat 6 g, fibre 3·5 g

3 BUZZ — per 25 g: sugar 16 g, fat 7 g, fibre 1 g

4 BOOM — per 20 g: sugar 15 g, fat 3·5 g, fibre 0·5 g

5c A

Change Machine A
fraction → decimal

75%, 54%, 8%, 25%, 80%, 63%, 0·1%, 20%

1/5

Change Machine B
percentage → decimal

1/2, 3/4, 7/10, 52/100, 1/4, 3/10, 1/5, 9/100

Change Machine C
fraction → percentage

0·23, 0·5, 0·25, 0·1, 0·49, 0·9, 0·33, 0·05

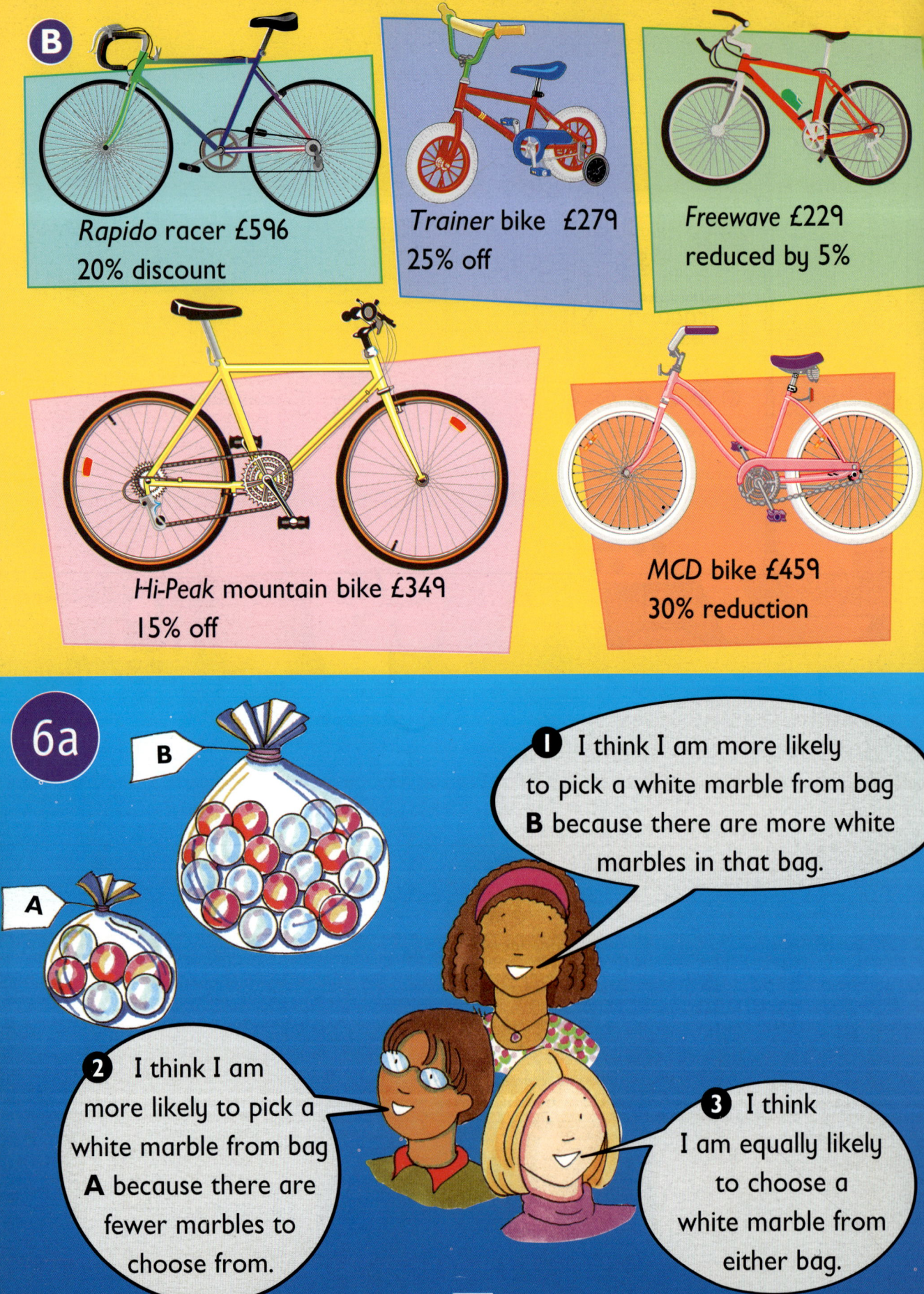

6b

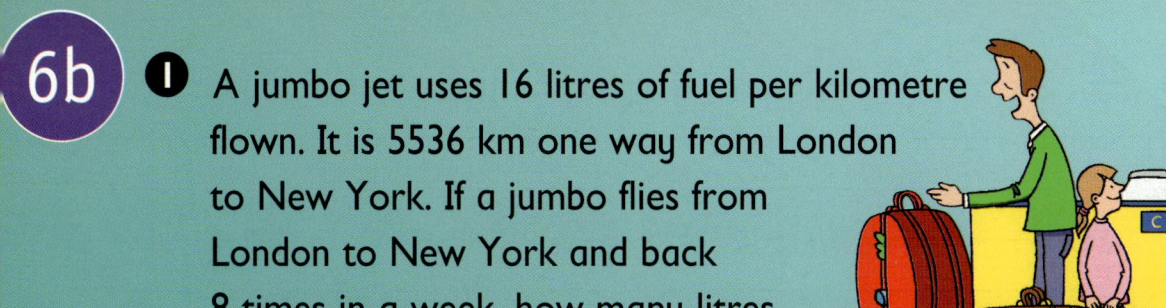

1 A jumbo jet uses 16 litres of fuel per kilometre flown. It is 5536 km one way from London to New York. If a jumbo flies from London to New York and back 8 times in a week, how many litres of fuel are used up?

2 A litre of fuel costs 6p. How much does it cost in fuel for a jumbo jet to make a return trip from London to New York?

3 The table below gives the number of passengers leaving and arriving at an airport over the course of a week. Do more people leave or arrive? How many more?

Day	Sunday	Monday	Tuesday	Wednesday	Thursday	Friday	Saturday
Arrive	21 789	34 673	18 602	14 771	17 239	20 694	23 990
Depart	22 539	36 882	17 303	15 006	18 421	21 560	22 976

4 It takes each person who arrives at the airport 45 seconds to go through passport control. There are 20 control counters. How long did it take altogether for the passengers who arrived on Sunday to get through passport control?

7a

Cycling accidents by age in London over one year

Source: London Accident Analysis Unit (1998)

Number of accidents (vertical axis, 0 to 800)

Age (years): 0–4, 5–9, 10–14, 15–19, 20–24, 25–29, 30–34, 35–39, 40–44, 45–49, 50–54, 55–59, 60–64, over 65

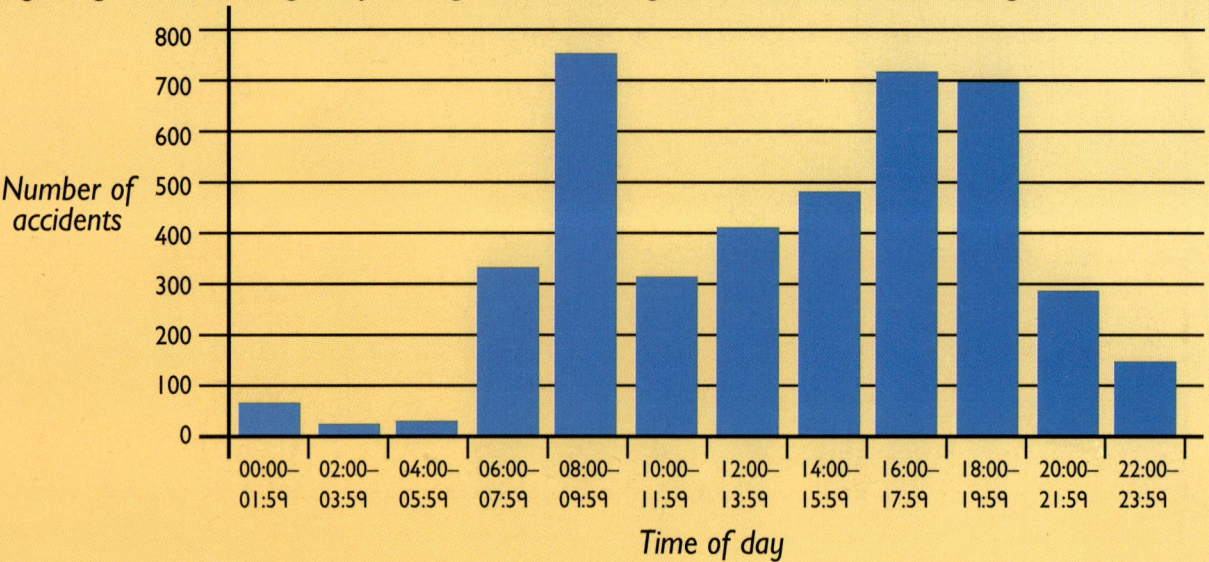

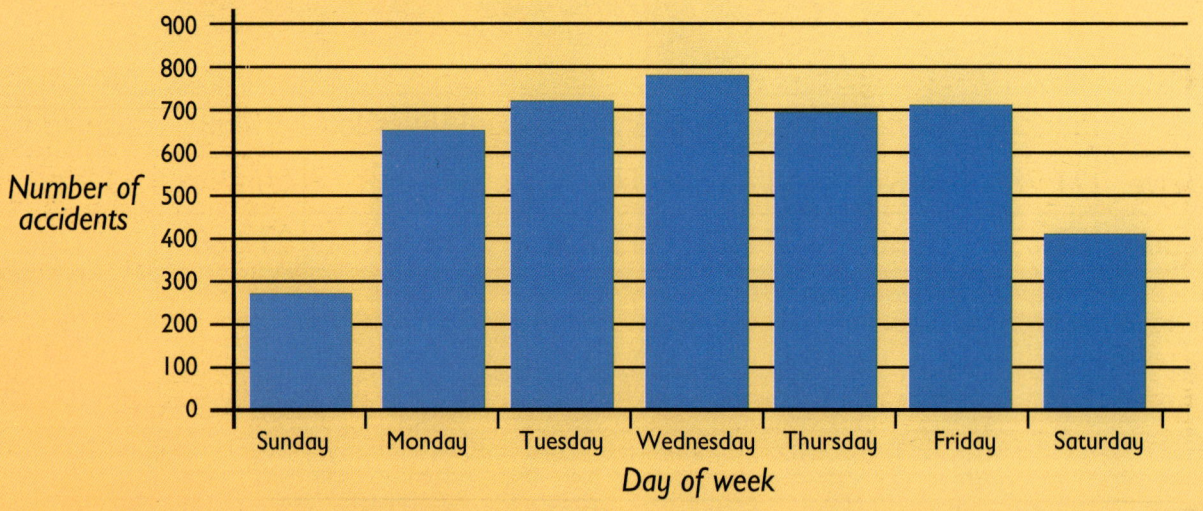

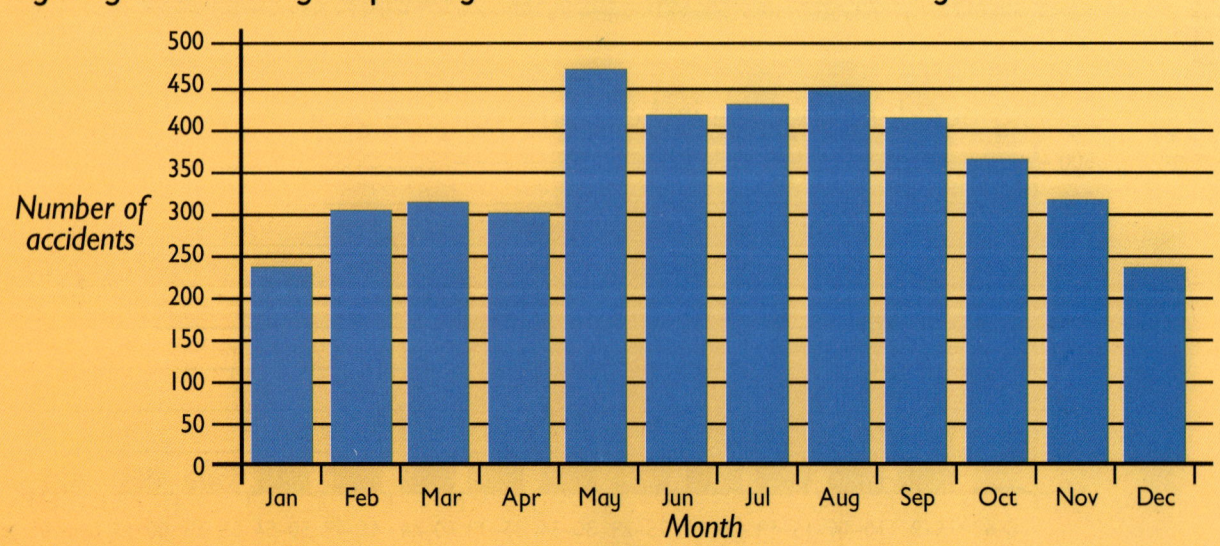

7b

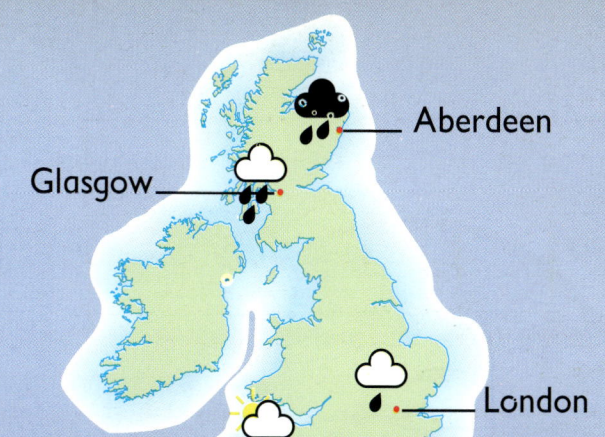

❶ Average monthly rainfall (in millimetres) from 1961 to 1990 in London and Glasgow

Month	Jan	Feb	Mar	Apr	May	Jun	Jul	Aug	Sep	Oct	Nov	Dec
London	53	36	48	44	52	52	45	52	50	59	55	58
Glasgow	110	74	83	50	63	60	62	82	112	115	110	105

❷ Average monthly rainfall (in millimetres) from 1961 to 1990 in Plymouth and Aberdeen

Month	Jan	Feb	Mar	Apr	May	Jun	Jul	Aug	Sep	Oct	Nov	Dec
Plymouth	115	92	86	57	62	57	54	70	78	96	100	118
Aberdeen	81	52	58	54	59	54	60	77	64	78	74	72

Estimated rainfall based on data obtained from the Met Office (http://www.met-office.gov.uk) statistics for: East Malling (London), Paisley (Glasgow), St Mawgan (Plymouth), Craibstone (Aberdeen).

8a

| Never true | Sometimes true | Always true |

❶ Squares have four axes of symmetry.

❷ Rectangles have two axes of symmetry.

❸ Triangles have four axes of symmetry.

❹ Parallelograms have no axes of symmetry.

❺ Trapeziums have one axis of symmetry.

8b

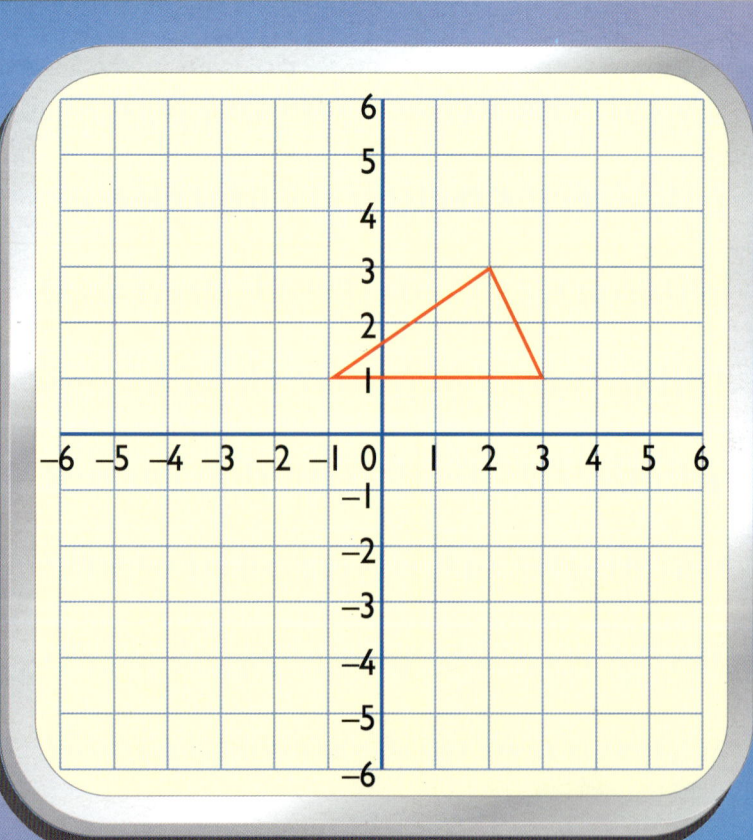

8c

1. 3 squares left.
2. 2 squares up.
3. 7 squares down.
4. 3 squares right and 2 squares down.

9a

1
8 m
10 m
2
10 m
6 m
3
4 m
6 m
4
8 m
13 m

9b

1
10 m
12 m
8 m
19 m
2
4 m
5 m
7 m
24 m
3
4 m
15 m
30 m
24 m
4
4 m
8 m
4 m
6 m
12 m
5
5 m
3 m
9 m
19 m
11 m

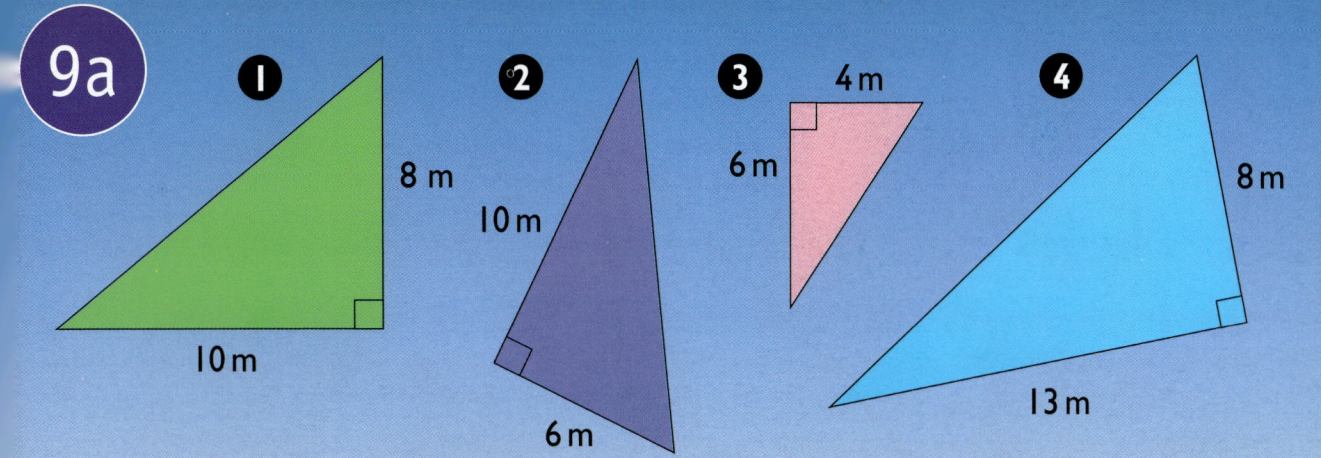

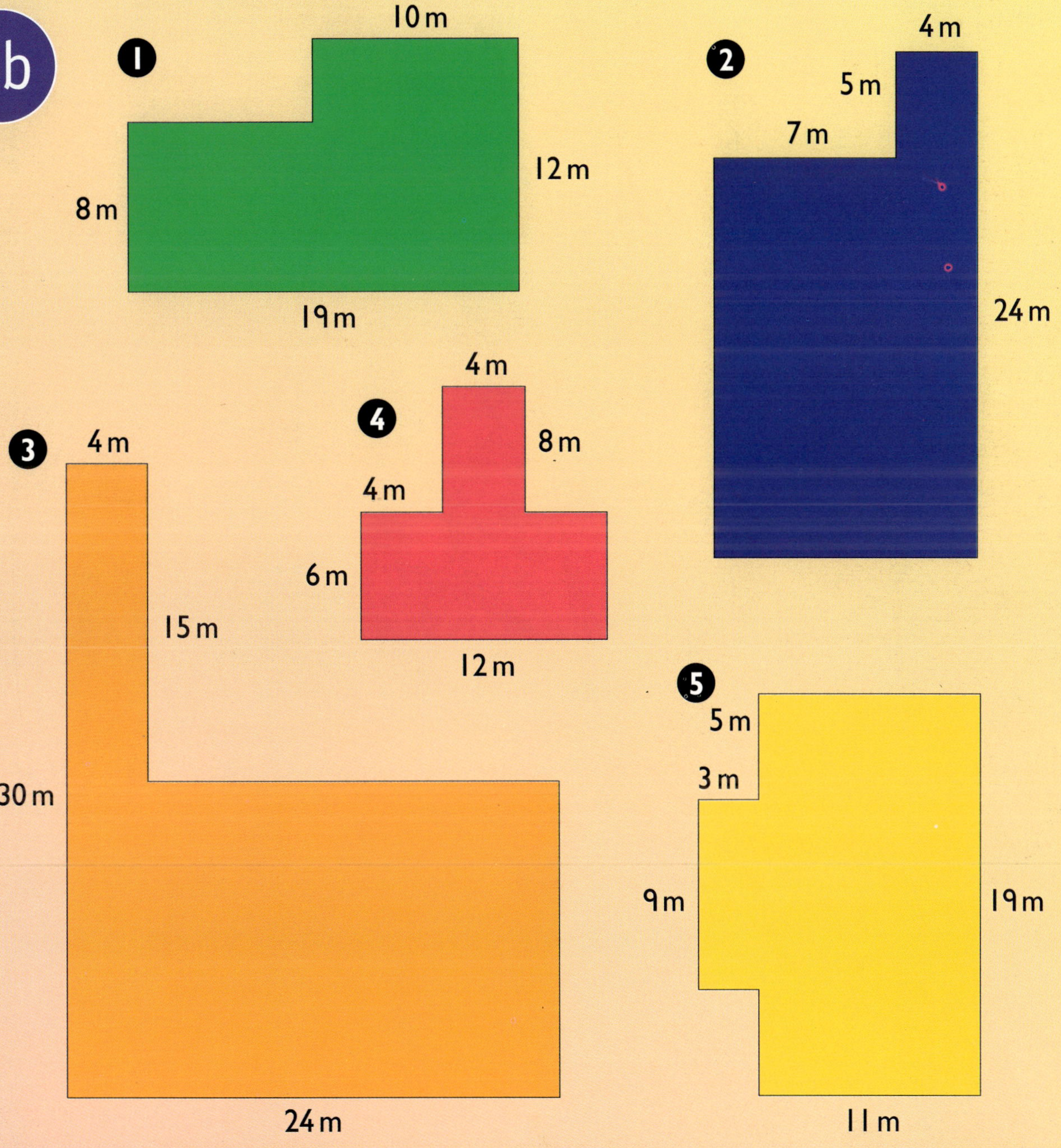

1 Jenny in Leeds picks up the telephone at 6:00 p.m. and rings her Aunt Lucy in New York. Aunt Lucy is eating when the phone rings. Which meal is she more likely to be eating, breakfast or lunch?

2 a Josie in Manchester sends a fax to her cousin in Sydney at 7:00 p.m. Is Josie's cousin likely to be awake when the fax arrives?

b Pat in Glasgow e-mails her son at work in Cape Town. She sends the e-mail at 11:00 a.m. Is her son likely to be at his work computer when the e-mail arrives?

3 a Ming in Beijing telephones her friend Susie in London. She knows that Susie goes to bed around 11:00 p.m. If it is 9:00 a.m in Beijing when Ming rings, is she likely to wake Susie?

b Miguel in Mexico City e-mails his friend Tony in Swansea. Miguel sends the e-mail when the time in Mexico City is 1:00 p.m. If Tony leaves work at 5:30 p.m. is he likely to get the e-mail before leaving work?

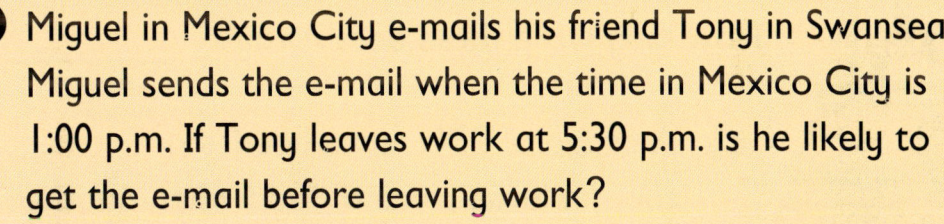

4 a Gulsham in Delhi sends a fax to her son Sanjit in Rio de Janeiro. She sends the fax when it is 8:00 p.m. in Delhi. Is Sanjit likely to be in his office to collect the fax when it arrives?

b Chuck in San Francisco telephones his friend Pierre in Paris. Chuck notices that the time is 4:00 p.m. in San Francisco when Pierre answers. Is Pierre likely to be woken up?

11

❶ There are 56 734 ants in an anthill. One day, 5402 go out foraging for food but 3788 return to the anthill. How many stay out to forage?

❷ On a warm summer's day, 3702 bees leave their hive in search of nectar. At the same time, another 1286 bees fly off from a neighbouring hive. The bees search together for 45 minutes. Then, after ten minutes collecting nectar, 2334 of the bees fly back to their hives, taking 55 minutes to get there. How long were these bees away?

❸ A group of 2341 dung beetles are struggling to carry a large piece of food when another 1547 beetles join them to help. Part of the food breaks off and is carried away by 1893 of the beetles. How many beetles are left to carry the rest of the food?

❹ A queen bee is surrounded by 6402 worker bees. In one day she lays 3408 eggs but only 2709 of these hatch. How many eggs did not hatch?

5 A group of 8721 woodlice are hiding under a log. Early one morning, 5675 of them crawl out from under the log to explore. A passer-by treads on them, crushing 2899. The remaining woodlice scuttle back under the log. How many are now under the log?

6 A group of 2400 ants get very excited at finding a dropped ice-cream cone. Unfortunately a quarter of them eat too much and die, and a third of them drown in the chocolate sauce. How many ants survive?

7 A team of 3480 ants are locked in battle with another team of 2765 ants over a leftover sandwich. After half an hour, 1784 of the ants run away and 2037 have been killed. How many ants are left to eat up the sandwich?

8 A swarm of 7891 flies lands on some over-ripe fruit. Each fly lays 3 eggs. How many eggs are laid in total?

12a

A

1. 56 65 74 83
2. 3 10 17 24
3. 14 35 56 77
4. 1·09 1·08 1·07 1·06
5. −441 −341 −241 −141
6. 9 700 9 400 9 100
7. 30 45 60 75
8. −120 −95 −70 −45
9. $1\frac{5}{8}$ $2\frac{1}{8}$ $2\frac{5}{8}$ $3\frac{1}{8}$
10. 0·5 0·75 1 1·25

B

1. 1 _ 13 _ 25
   1 _ _ 13 _ _ 25
   1 _ _ _ 13 _ _ _ 25
   1 _ _ _ _ _ 13 _ _ _ _ _ 25

2. 5 _ 17 _ 29
   5 _ _ 17 _ _ 29
   5 _ _ _ 17 _ _ _ 29
   5 _ _ _ _ _ 17 _ _ _ _ _ 29

3. 4 _ 28 _ 52
   4 _ _ 28 _ _ 52
   4 _ _ _ 28 _ _ _ 52
   4 _ _ _ _ _ 28 _ _ _ _ _ 52

4. −22 _ −10 _ 2
   −22 _ _ −10 _ _ 2
   −22 _ _ _ −10 _ _ _ 2
   −22 _ _ _ _ _ −10 _ _ _ _ _ 2

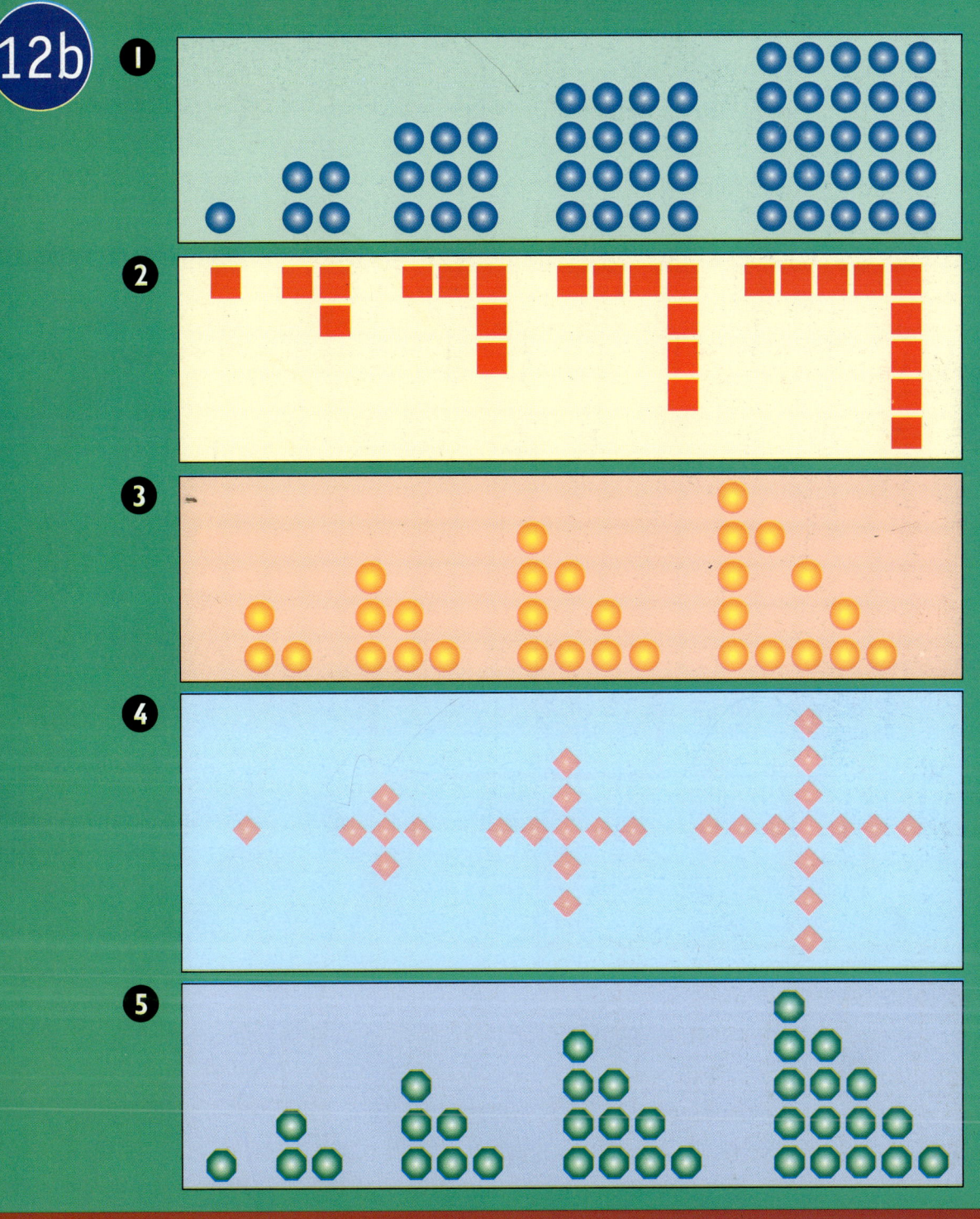

12c

1. Which numbers appear most times?
2. Which numbers appear only once?
3. Which numbers appear twice only?
4. Which numbers appear three times?
5. Which numbers do not appear at all?

13a

A
1. −45, 6, 38, −5, −50, 24
2. 1, −72, 67, −8, −12, 54
3. −3, −91, 82, −56, −4, 7
4. 90, −14, 5, −3, −83, −97

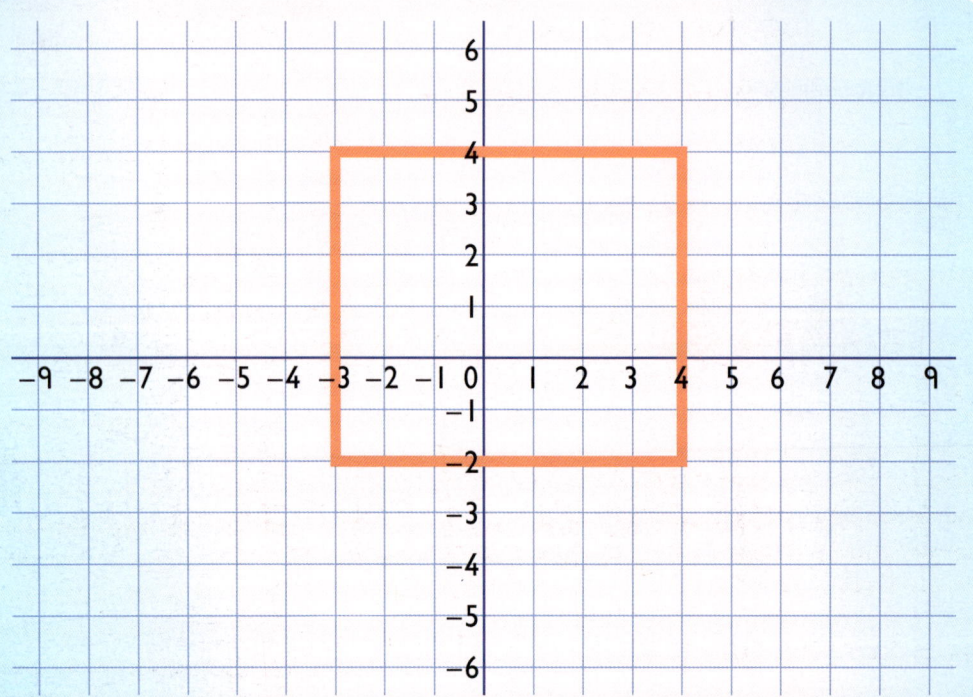

1. (−2, 2) (6, 2) (6, −1) (−2, −1)
2. (−3, 5) (3, 3) (3, −1) (−3, −2)
3. (5, 5) (5, −2) (−2, −2)
4. (5, 7) (−5, 7) (−5, −7) (5, −7)
5. (8, −2) (8, −5) (−2, −5) (−2, −2)
6. (8, −2) (0, 5) (−8, −2)
7. (2, 9) (−2, 9) (0, 2)

13b A

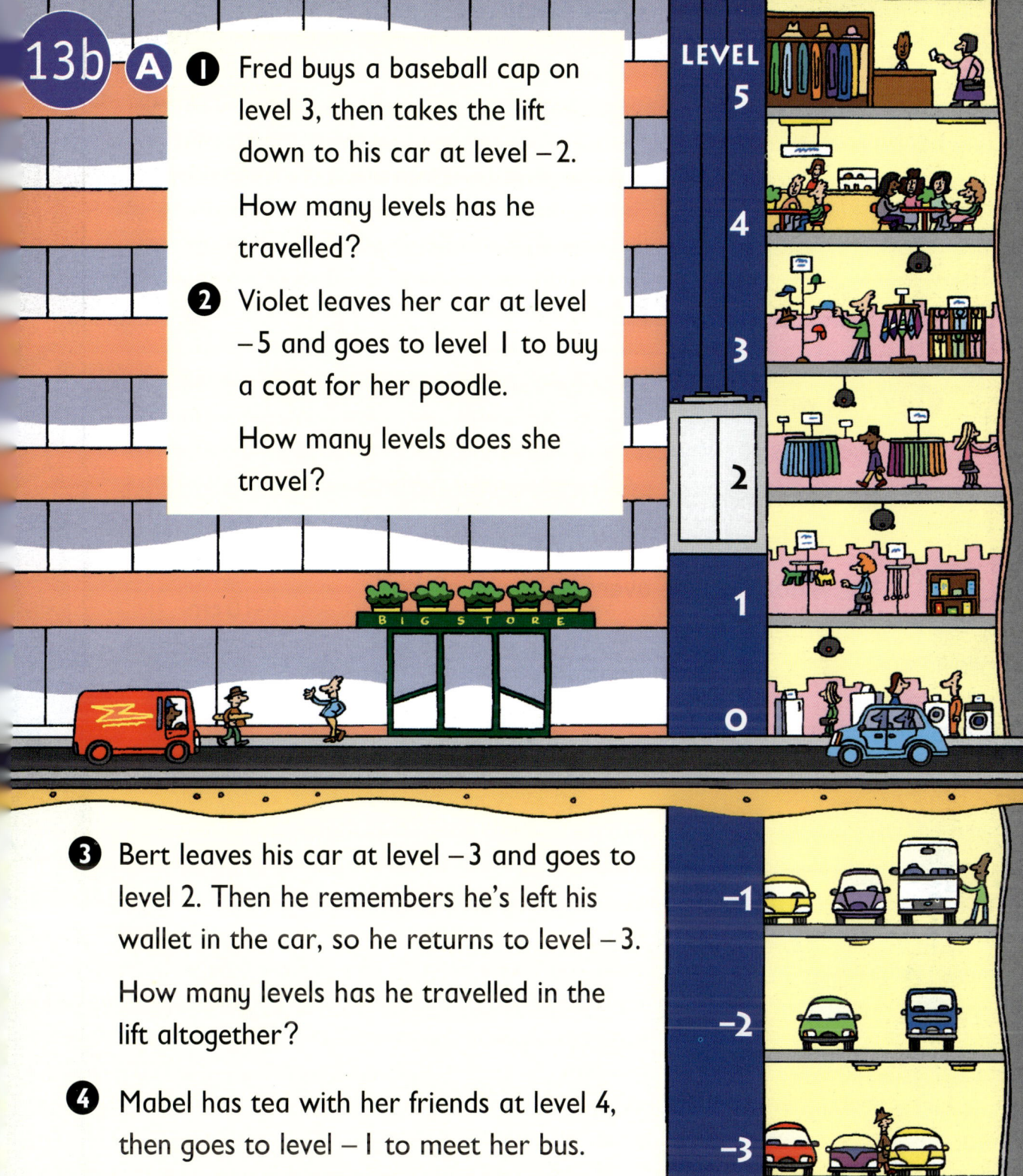

1 Fred buys a baseball cap on level 3, then takes the lift down to his car at level −2.

How many levels has he travelled?

2 Violet leaves her car at level −5 and goes to level 1 to buy a coat for her poodle.

How many levels does she travel?

3 Bert leaves his car at level −3 and goes to level 2. Then he remembers he's left his wallet in the car, so he returns to level −3.

How many levels has he travelled in the lift altogether?

4 Mabel has tea with her friends at level 4, then goes to level −1 to meet her bus.

How many levels did she go down?

5 Minnie gets her coat from the staff cloakroom on level 5, and goes down to level −4 to get the staff coach. How many levels is this?

B The water in the lock is measured by how much it rises and falls. The 'zero' level is the normal level of the water, which is 10 metres. Each week the gauge reading is recorded. Copy and complete the table.

Week 1	Week 2	Week 3	Week 4	Week 5	Week 6	Week 7	Week 8
+10 cm	0	−10 cm	−20 cm	−30 cm	−20 cm	−10 cm	0
10·1 m	10 m						

1. What was the highest the water level rose to?
2. What was the lowest level the water fell to?
3. What was the greatest difference in the levels throughout the two months?
4. What was the average height of the water throughout the two months?

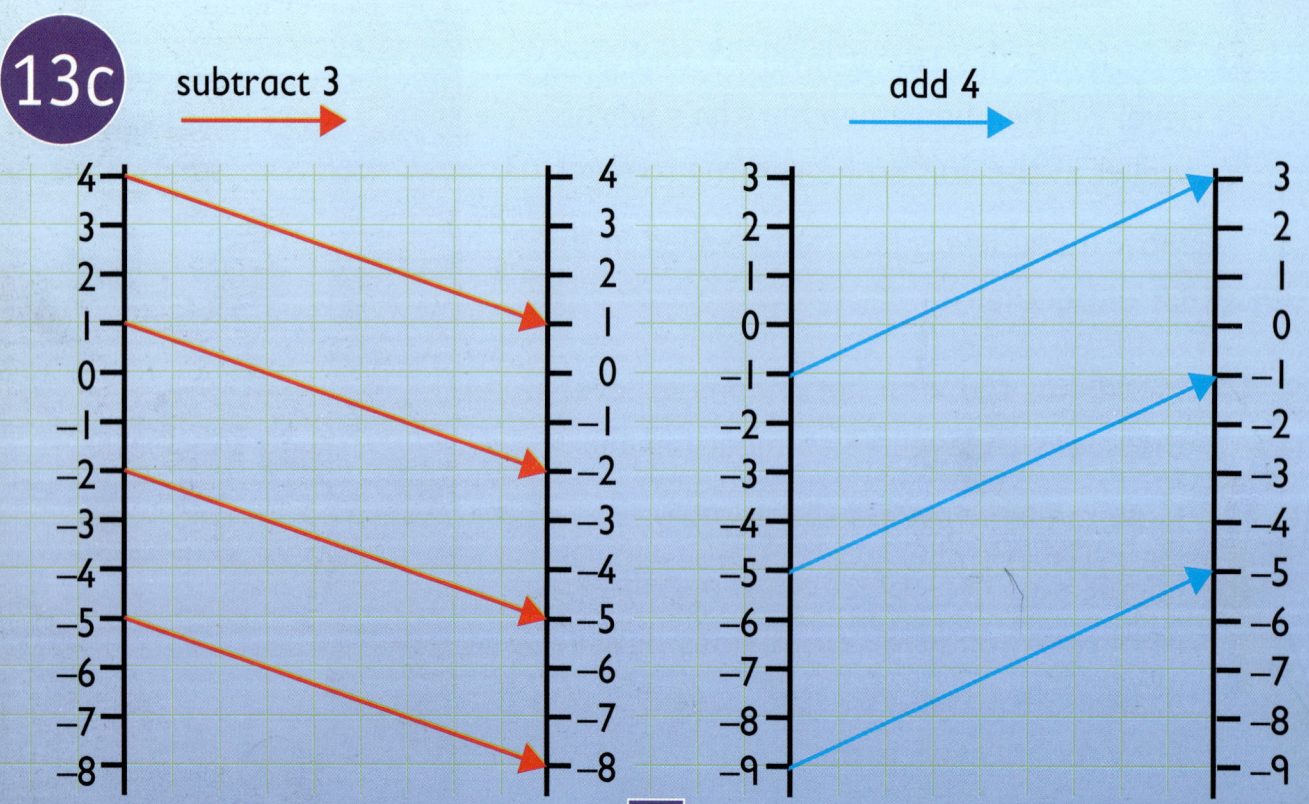

13c

subtract 3

add 4

14a

| Set 1 | 9 | 21 | 29 | 41 | 49 | 51 | 61 | 99 | 101 |
| Set 2 | 8 | 13 | 17 | 25 | 34 | 42 | 46 | 55 | 58 |

14b

A
1. (□ × □) × 6 = 36
2. (□ × □) ÷ 3 = 10
3. (□ × □) × (□ × □) = 64

1 2 2 3 4 5 6 8

B
1. 1 + 2 × 3 + 4 × 5
2. 2 × 4 × 3 × 5
3. 2 × 6 ÷ 3 × 2
4. 2 × 3 + 6 + 4 × 5

C
15 18 42 24 36 32

15a

1. 267 ÷ 13
2. 682 ÷ 44
3. 784 ÷ 56
4. 456 ÷ 27
5. 312 ÷ 36

15b

1. 672 ÷ 31
2. 378 ÷ 34
3. 378 ÷ 18
4. 695 ÷ 23
5. 597 ÷ 38

```
              21  r21
          31)672
20 x 31  - 620
             52
1 x 31  -    31
             21
```

15c

1. 1·35 ÷ 3
2. 2·35 ÷ 5
3. 6·36 ÷ 6
4. 4·68 ÷ 6
5. 6·88 ÷ 8
6. 8·33 ÷ 7

16a

Flag	Currency	£1 buys	£1 costs
🇦🇺	Australian dollar	2.471	2.673
🇨🇦	Canadian dollar	2.131	2.306
🇨🇾	Cypriot pound	0.908	0.980
🇩🇰	Danish krone	11.805	12.776
🇬🇷	Greek drachma	533.804	577.197
🇭🇰	Hong Kong dollar	11.210	12.137
🇮🇱	Israeli new shekel	5.842	6.320
🇲🇹	Maltese lira	0.638	0.688
🇳🇴	Norwegian krone	12.843	13.896
🇸🇦	Saudi Arabian riyal	5.391	5.836
🇿🇦	South African rand	10.000	10.812
🇨🇭	Swiss franc	2.451	2.652
🇹🇷	Turkish lira	925 378.256	1 000 836.975
🇺🇸	US dollar	1.437	1.556

1 David buys £7 worth of Cypriot pounds. How much money in Cypriot pounds does he have?

2 Shari's mother buys a car when they go to live in Israel. It costs 9270 shekels. How much money can this buy in pounds sterling?

3 Dodi has 819 Swiss francs left after his holiday in Switzerland. How much will he have when he changes it into pounds?

4 Floella is going on holiday to Greece. She has £17 to change into drachmas. How much money in drachmas will she have to spend?

5 Della has 678 Danish kroner left in her purse after her weekend trip to Copenhagen. She changes the money at the port for British pounds. How much money does she have in pounds?

16b

Mrs Smith went to her local shop. This is her till receipt.

1 How much did each packet of biscuits cost?

2 There are 12 biscuits in each pack. What is the price of each biscuit?

3 The Smith family use 3 litres of milk each week. How much do they spend each week on milk?

4 The apples were for Mrs Smith's neighbour. How much did Mrs Smith's own items cost?

```
COTTAGE STORES
SOUTHFIELD

                        12.11.2000

2 l MILK                      1.32
2 kg APPLES (8 PACK)   1.29
1 kg PLAIN FLOUR              88
5 PACKETS BISCUITS      2.90
6 EGGS                        96
450g SUGAR                    79
                        _____
TOTAL                   £ 8.14
```

5 Did the apples cost more or less than 16p each?

6 Mr Smith uses some of the ingredients to make biscuits.
He needs to buy: 70 grams of flour
2 eggs
225 grams of sugar

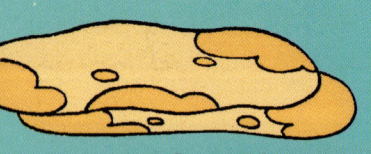

Is it cheaper to make or buy biscuits if the recipe makes 16 biscuits?

16c

1 263 ÷ ☐ = 10·52

2 37 ☆ 21 + 223 = 1000

3 36 × 18 ☆ 27 = 675

4 476 ☆ (2040 ÷ 24) = 391

5 323 × ☐ = 15 181

6 9776 ☆ ☐ + 18 = 70

7 ☐ ☆ 1·7 = 8

17a

A

1) $\frac{11}{16}$ $\frac{1}{4}$ $\frac{7}{8}$ $\frac{1}{2}$

2) $\frac{7}{10}$ $\frac{4}{5}$ $\frac{3}{4}$ $\frac{1}{2}$

3) $1\frac{3}{10}$ $1\frac{4}{15}$ $1\frac{2}{5}$ $1\frac{1}{6}$

4) $2\frac{1}{4}$ $3\frac{3}{4}$ $1\frac{1}{2}$ $3\frac{3}{8}$

B

Car	Length (m)	Width (m)	Height (m)
Rambler	4·152	1·735	1·269
Focal	4·3	1·8	1·5
Scorcher	4·005	1·818	1·534
Rev	4·15	1·69	1·31
Marathon	4·17	1·77	1·96
Roadster	4·105	1·832	1·096

17b

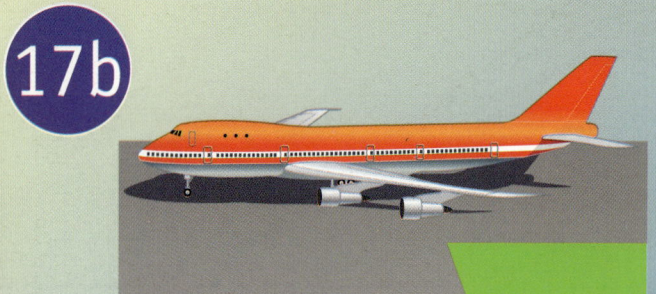

Boeing 747
length 70·66 m
wingspan 59·64 m

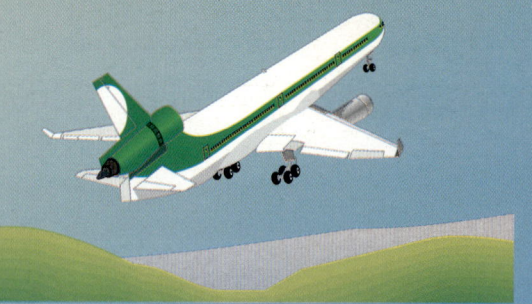

McDonnell Douglas DC 10
length 55·35 m
wingspan 40·42 m

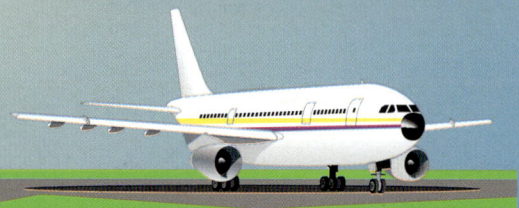

Airbus
length 54·20 m
wingspan 47·35 m

Boeing 767
length 48·50 m
wingspan 47·60 m

18a

1
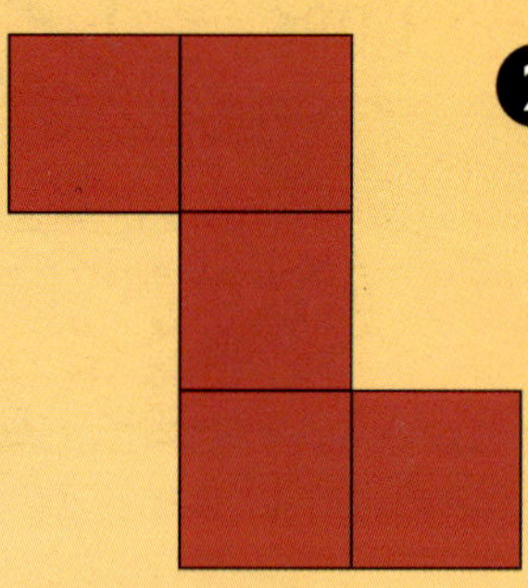

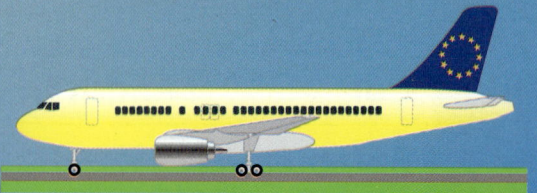

2
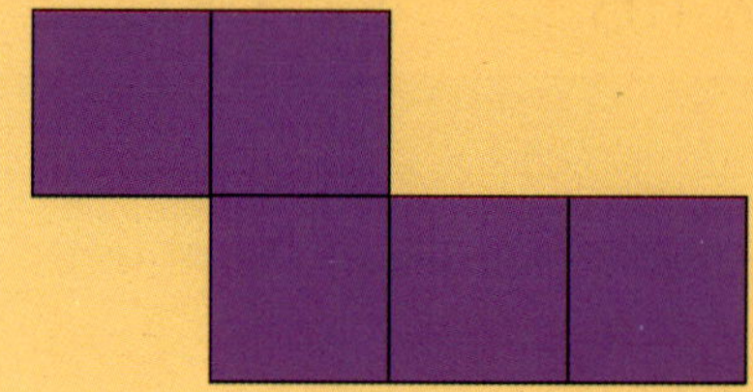

3
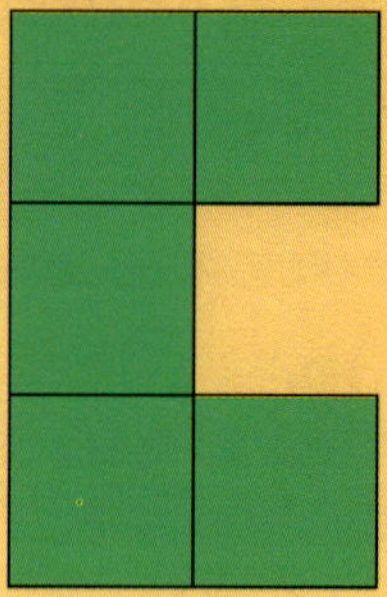

4
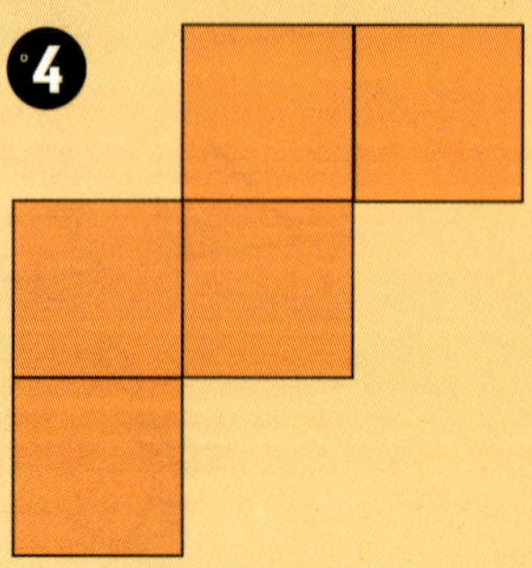

5
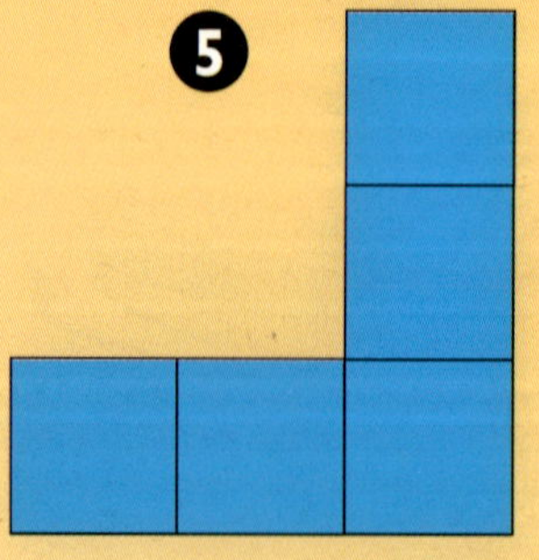

6
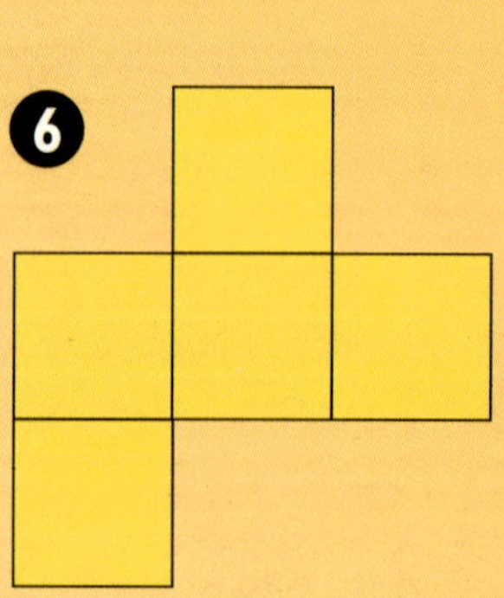

18b

A

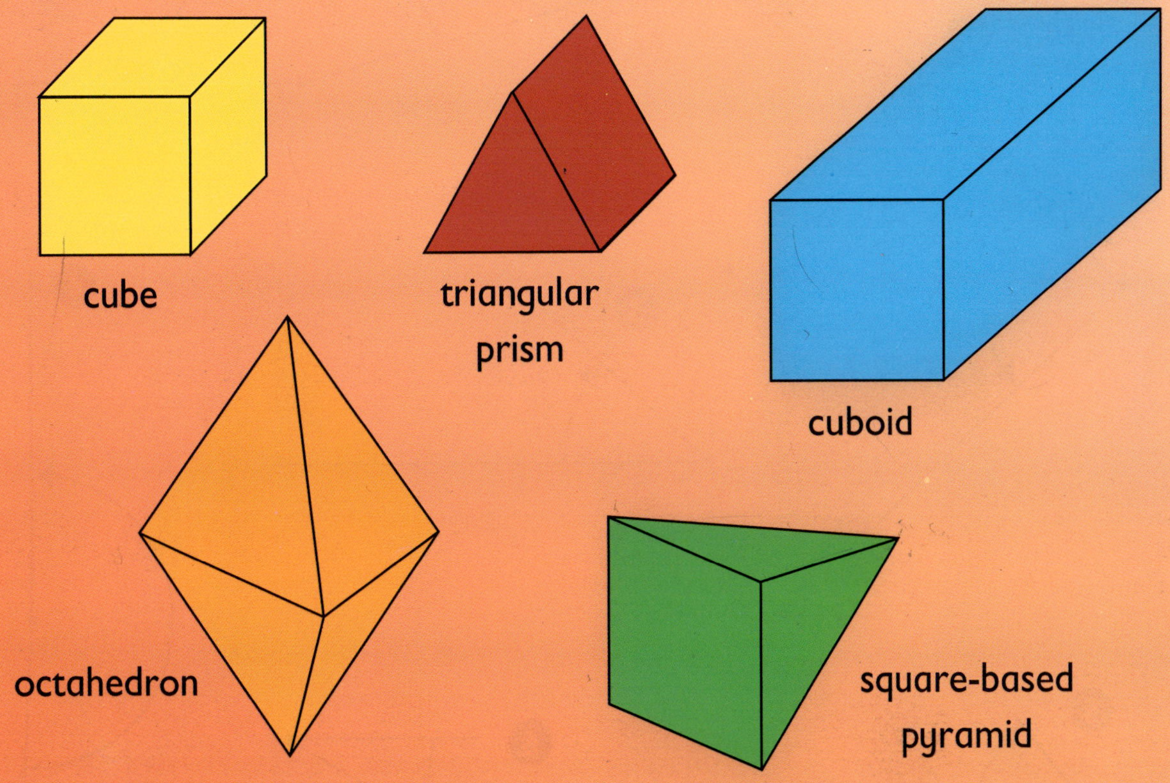

- cube
- triangular prism
- cuboid
- octahedron
- square-based pyramid

B

1.
2.
3.
4.
5.
6.
7.

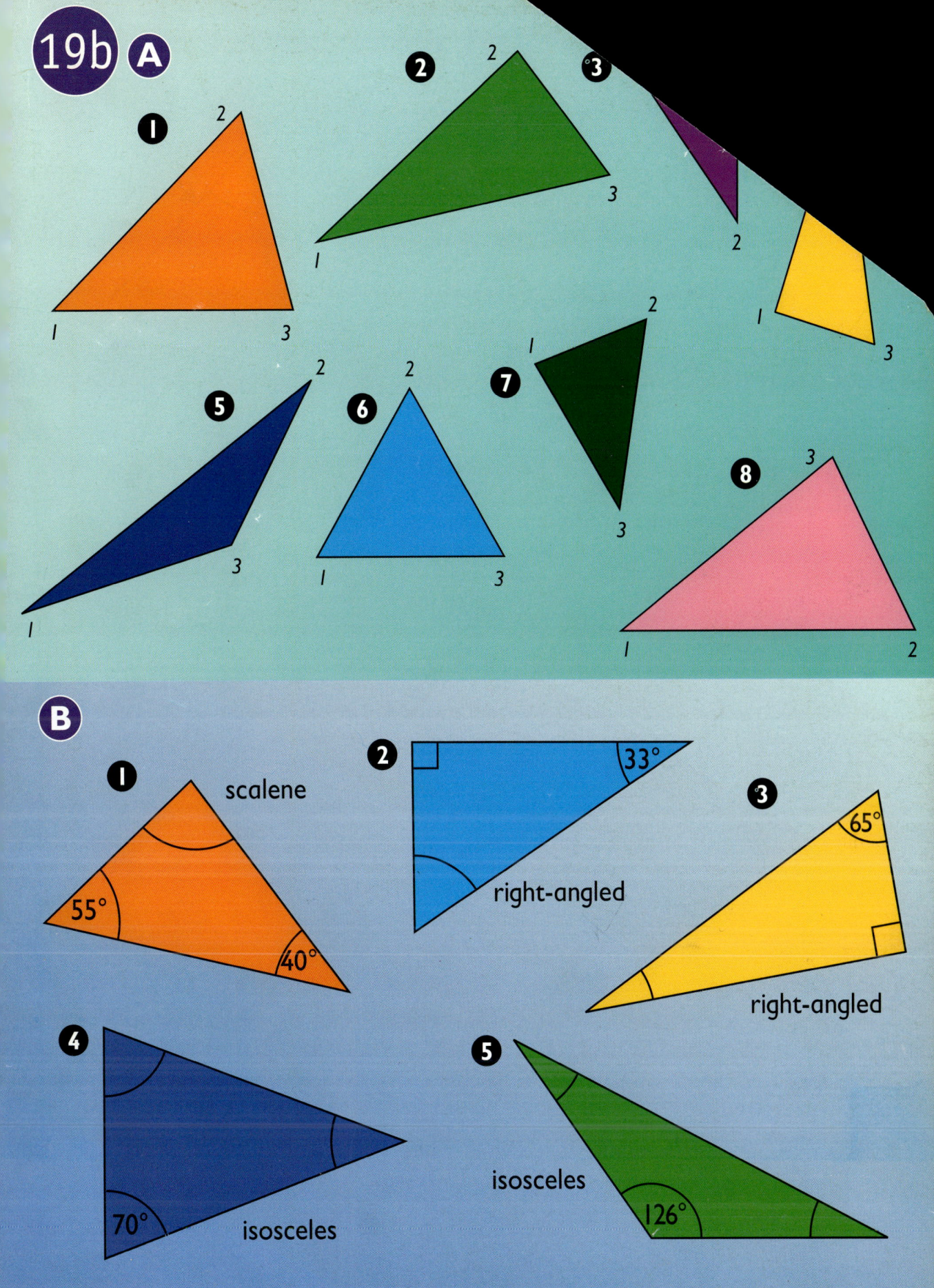

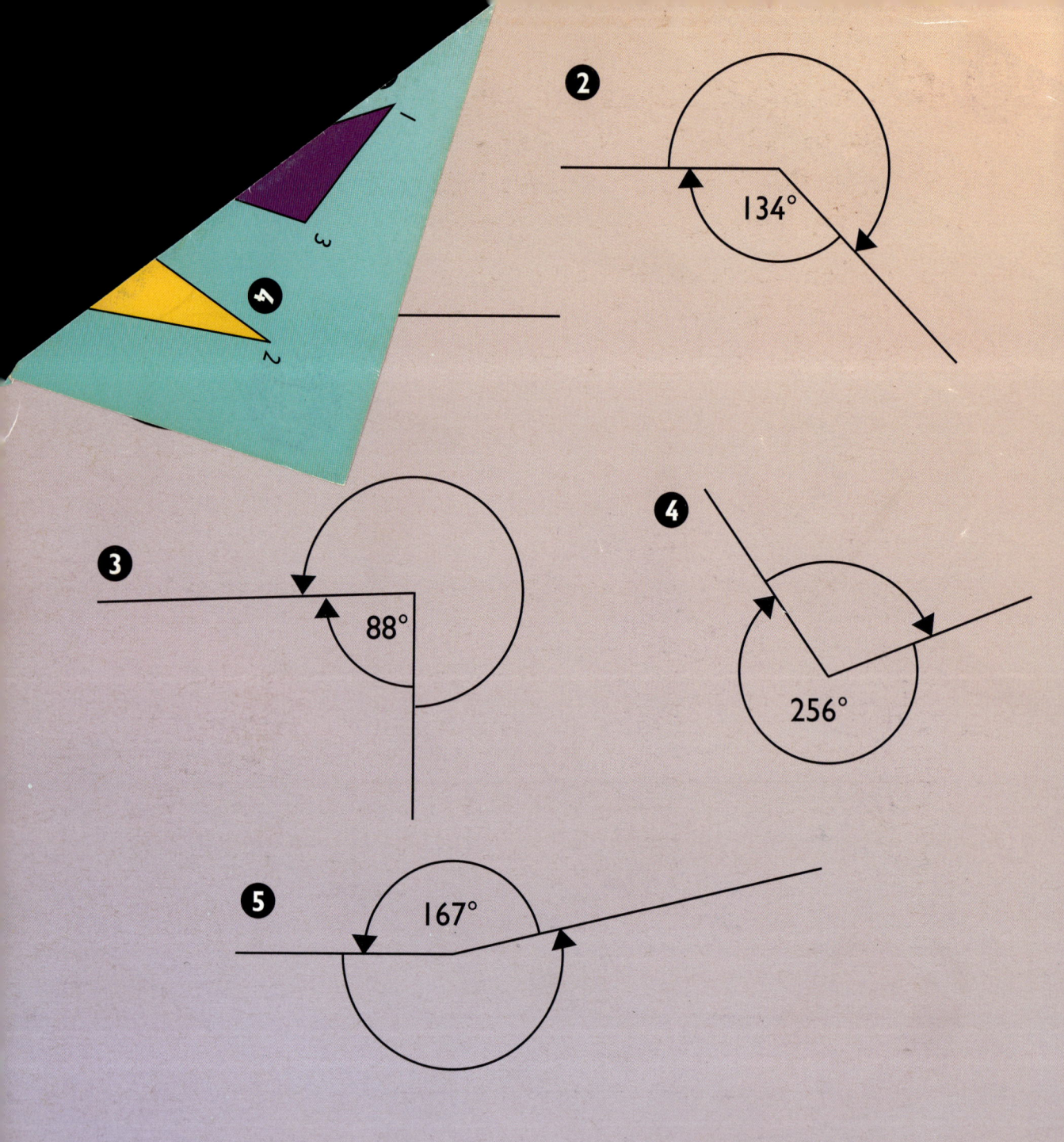

21a

1 Nancy bought a new pedometer for her bike to find out how far she cycled each week. On Thursday she cycled 1·6 km, on Saturday she cycled 28·47 kilometres, on Sunday she cycled 12·08 km, and on Monday she cycled 800 m. How many kilometres did she travel that week?

2 Erhan was worried about how much luggage he was taking on holiday. His suitcase weighed 24·53 kilograms, his rucksack weighed 13·8 kilograms, and his carrier bag weighed 450 g. How much did his luggage weigh altogether?

3 Jeremy's aquarium needs cleaning out. The aquarium holds 5·5 litres of water. Jeremy put in 2 l 550 ml of water, then 1 l 680 ml. He has a 1·5 l full jug of water. Is that enough water to fill the tank to the 5·5 l mark?

4 Mabel has a roll of chicken wire to make a rabbit run. The chicken wire is 2·5 metres long. Mabel cuts off two lengths, one 85 cm long and the other 1·25 m long. Has she got enough chicken wire left to repair the 50 cm hole in the fence?

5 Mandy is saving up for a CD player costing £97.99. She gets £34.62 for her birthday, she saves £27.04, she finds 84p but loses 35p down the back of a cushion. She earns £3.25 for cleaning the windows. How much more has she got to save up?

21b A

① 9006 − 6487	② 513 + 477
③ 21·3 − 1·9	④ 3·8 − 3·78
⑤ 0·87 + 0·2	⑥ 0·6 − 0·41
⑦ 3400 + 6700	⑧ 7300 − 4700
⑨ 46 + 19 + 34	⑩ 41 + 39 − 67

B

Error	I think I keyed in…	The display showed…
① A digit has been left out	3008 − 26 =	282
② A wrong unit digit has been entered	777 ÷ 21 =	28.777777
③ Two digits were reversed	73.67 − 34.58 =	30.09
④ A number was entered twice	11 × 35 =	38885
⑤ A wrong operation was entered	2001 × 12 =	1989
⑥ The decimal point was put in the wrong place	13.6 + 3.53 =	4.89
⑦ The equals sign was pressed twice	1326 ÷ 51 =	0.5098039

22a

Museum	Opening times		
	Mon–Fri	Sat	Sun
Bank of England Museum	10:00–17:00	closed	closed
Beaulieu Car Museum	10:00–17:00	10:00–17:00	10:00–17:00
British Museum	10:00–17:00	10:00–17:00	12:00–18:00
Cardiff Techniquest Museum	09:30–16:30	10:30–17:00	10:30–17:00
Edinburgh Royal Observatory	10:00–17:00	10:00–17:00	12:00–17:00
Florence Nightingale Museum	10:00–17:00	11:30–16:30	11:30–16:30
Ironbridge Gorge Museum	10:00–17:00	10:00–17:00	10:00–17:00
Madame Tussaud's	09:00–17:30	09:00–17:30	09:00–17:30
Natural History Museum	10:00–17:50	10:00–17:50	11:00–17:50
Westonzoyland Pumping Station	Thursday only 14:00–20:00	closed	14:00–17:00

❶ How many hours per week is each museum open for?

❷ Jim Green works from Wednesday to Sunday at one of these museums, from opening time to closing time. He works 34 hours per week. Which museum might he work for?

❸ Uncle John, aged 36, took his five-year-old nephew and two seven-year-old nieces out to a museum on Sunday. He had change from £10 when he bought the tickets. Which museum might they have gone to?

❹ Mrs Robinson, aged 42, took six children to the Florence Nightingale Museum. What change did she have from £30 when she bought the tickets?

Admission charges

Adult	Child	OAP	Student
free	free	free	free
£9.25	£6.50	£8.00	£8.00
free	free	free	free
£5.50	£3.80	£3.80	£3.80
£3.50	£2.50	£2.00	£2.00
£4.80	£3.60	£3.60	£3.60
£10.00	£6.00	£9.00	£6.00
£11.50	£8.00	£9.00	£11.50
£7.50	free	free	£4.50
£3.00	£2.00	£2.50	£3.00

5 Kim is at school. His sister is a student at college. His grandad is a pensioner. Instead of going to Madame Tussaud's, they all go to the Natural History Museum to save money. How much extra money do they now have to spend on pizzas?

6 If Cardiff Techniquest Museum admits 100 000 visitors each year, what is the maximum amount of admission charges the museum could collect? What is the minimum amount? Estimate how much the museum would really collect from 100 000 people.

22b

1. 6 * 3 * 3 = 27
2. 8 * 2 * 8 * 4 = 48
3. 9 * 1 * 6 = 48
4. 4 * 5 * 3 * 2 = 34
5. 5 * 6 * 3 * 7 = 70
6. 7 * 7 * 2 * 2 = 102
7. 9 * 9 * 5 * 7 = 42
8. 7 * 9 * 5 = 68
9. 10 * 2 * 5 = 25
10. 3 * 8 * 2 * 2 = 96

23a

23b

A

1. 1347 × 349 = 470 103
2. 566 × 628 = 355 489
3. 847 × 152 = 128 744
4. 248 × 532 = 131 936
5. 356 × 163 = 58 029
6. 59 × 877 = 51 744
7. 952 × 243 = 231 336
8. 487 × 538 = 262 007

24a

1. 1·8 + 0·6
2. 170 + 750
3. 64·8 ÷ 8
4. 3·6 + 4·8 + 1·4
5. 17 × 51
6. 670 + 380
7. 24 × 25
8. 385 − 144
9. 0·8 + 0·45
10. 2·8 ÷ 2
11. 768 − 372
12. 2002 − 750
13. 41 + □ + 39 = 96
14. 17·5% of £8240
15. 0·1 × 32
16. 38 × 8
17. 26 × 15
18. 7000 − 3875
19. 8 × □ = 13·6
20. □ ÷ 2 = 2·4

A

true false

1. 47 is a prime number.

2. The lowest common multiple of 6 and 4 is 24.

3. $15 \div \tfrac{1}{2} = 30$

4. $14 \cdot 786 \times 100 = 1478 \cdot 6$

5. $17 \div 8 = 8 \div 17$

6. 304 is divisible by 4.

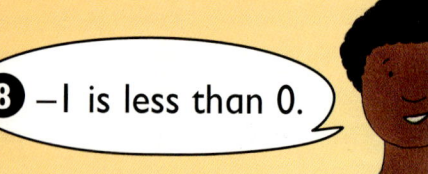
7. 164 is a multiple of 3.

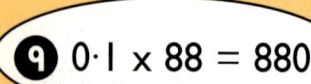
8. -1 is less than 0.

9. $0 \cdot 1 \times 88 = 880$

10. The temperature is $-15°C$ and it drops by $2°C$ to $-13°C$.

11. $\tfrac{2}{5}$ is equivalent to 40%.

12. $0 \cdot 67$ is larger than $0 \cdot 8$.

 ❶ Prime numbers are odd.

 ❷ Multiplying a number by another number makes the first number larger.

❸ When you multiply any number by 100 you move the digits two places to the left.

 ❹ To multiply by 25, multiply by 100 and divide by 4.

❺ Triangular numbers are odd.

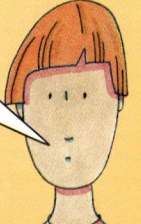 ❻ A square number is the sum of two consecutive triangular numbers.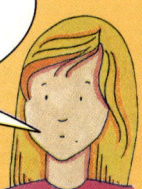

❼ The square of a number is double that number.

 ❽ Dividing a number by another number makes the first number smaller.

❾ If you add two negative numbers you get a positive number.

 ❿ Dividing a whole number by a half makes the number twice as big.

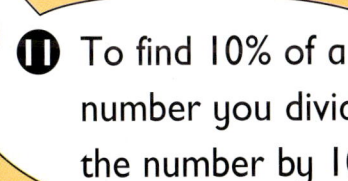 ⓫ To find 10% of a number you divide the number by 10.

⓬ A factor of 12 is a number that will divide by 12 exactly.

Rigby Paper Mill

The paper mill produces about 250 000 tonnes of paper per year.

One roll of paper weighs about 20 tonnes.

The paper mill produces about 1000 metres of paper per minute.

Each roll is 5 metres wide.

One metre of paper 5 metres wide weighs 500 grams.

The paper mill works non-stop, 24 hours per day, 7 days per week. One week per year the machines are shut down and serviced, and stop producing paper.

One ream of paper contains 500 sheets of paper.

One ream of paper weighs 2·5 kilograms.

One tonne is 1000 kilograms.

The average person in the UK uses 200 kilograms of paper per year.

1. About how many rolls of paper per year does Rigby Paper Mill produce?
2. About how many rolls of paper per day does Rigby Paper Mill produce?
3. What does 1000 m of paper weigh, roughly?
4. About what weight of paper can the paper mill produce in a second?
5. How long is a roll of paper?
6. How long, approximately, does it take to produce a roll of paper?
7. How many reams of paper can the paper mill cut from one roll of paper?
8. How many sheets of paper does the average person in the UK use in a year?

25b

A

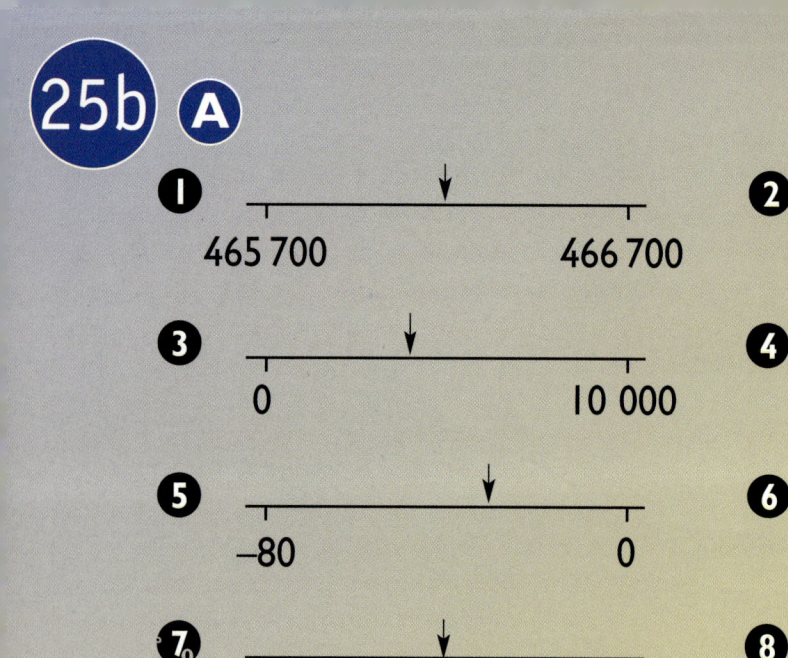

B

1 5087 + 972 6000 + 1000 5000 + 950 5000 + 1000 5100 + 1000

2 £36.80 + £58.80 £35.00 + £60.00 £36.00 + £60.00 £35.00 + £55.00 £37.00 + £60.00

3 51.2 − 39.8 51 − 39 51 − 40 50 − 39 512 − 398

4 9.09 × 4.93 10 × 5 10 × 4 9 × 5 9 × 4

25c

A

Number	Rounded to the nearest 10	Rounded to the nearest 100	Rounded to the nearest 1000	Rounded to the nearest 10 000	Rounded to the nearest 100 000	Rounded to the nearest 1 000 000
758 732						
678 941						
1 234 876						
2 957 365						
8 175 402						

B

1. The number of slices of bread in a loaf.
2. The number of matches in a matchbox.
3. The number of paperclips in a box.
4. The population of a country.
5. The height in metres of Mount Everest.
6. The distance in kilometres from Leeds to New York.
7. The distance in kilometres from the Earth to the Moon.
8. The distance in kilometres to the centre of the Earth.
9. The number of years ago dinosaurs last lived on Earth.
10. The speed in kilometres per hour of a peregrine falcon.

C

1 Six children can sit round each dining table. How many dining tables do we need for 20 children?

2 CDs cost £6. How many CDs can I buy with £20?

3 Pedigree hamsters cost £12. Jim has saved £68. How many hamsters can he buy?

4 There are 240 people going on a school outing. Coaches seat 45 people. How many coaches should the school book?

26a

1 207 ÷ 6
2 135 ÷ 20
3 405 ÷ 10
4 432 ÷ 100
5 90 ÷ 40
6 746 ÷ 8
7 289 ÷ 4
8 752 ÷ 5
9 90 ÷ 12
10 694 ÷ 8

26b

1. Captain Margaret bought 8 metres of plank. She needs lengths of 275 cm for each person who has to walk the plank. How many lengths can she cut?

2. Margaret and her crew capture 8000 gold doubloons. Each sack can hold 275 doubloons. How many sacks does Captain Margaret need to hold all the doubloons?

3. The pirates have found 2500 pearls. Each treasure-chest can hold 450 pearls. How many treasure-chests are needed to hold all the pearls?

4. The Dunsailin home for retired pirates has raised £2500 to buy new parrots. A new parrot costs £450. How many parrots can Dunsailin buy?

5. The pirate fleet can carry 4500 pirates on all its ships. Each ship can carry 285 pirates. How many ships must the fleet have to carry all 4500 pirates?

6. The printer has printed 4500 'wanted' leaflets. Each box can hold 285 leaflets. How many boxes does the printer need to hold all 4500 leaflets?

26c

1. $8.8 \times 100 = \square$
2. $\square \div 100 = 0.8$
3. One tenth of 43
4. $6.37 \times 10 = \square$
5. $\square \div 10 = 0.7$
6. $\square \times 2 = 1.4$
7. $0.73 \times \square = 73$
8. $5.3 \times \square = 21.2$
9. One hundredth of 82
10. $48 \div 10 = \square$
11. $\square \times 2 = 1.8$
12. One hundredth of 6
13. $0.77 \times 2 = \square$
14. One tenth of 9
15. $4.7 \times 6 = \square$
16. Double 0.86
17. Halve 0.3
18. $0.8 \times 4 = \square$
19. $\square \times 7 = 9.8$
20. $0.3 \div \square = 0.15$

27a

A
1. ☐ × 2 = 1·6
2. 0·45 × 2
3. 0·95 × 2
4. 0·36 × 2
5. ☐ × 2 = 1·66
6. 0·98 × 2
7. 0·87 × 2
8. ☐ × 2 = 1·94

B
1. 3·7 × 5
2. 7·2 × ☐ = 50·4
3. 6·3 × 9
4. ☐ × 6 = 14·4
5. 5·7 × ☐ = 17·1
6. ☐ × 9 = 14·4

27b

1. 261 × 24
2. 432 × 53
3. 655 × 27
4. 765 × 46
5. 676 × 74
6. 987 × 86

28a

1) | 1·47 | 1·407 | 7·014 | 4·701 |

2) | $6\frac{83}{100}$ | $8\frac{36}{1000}$ | $38\frac{6}{100}$ | $3\frac{608}{1000}$ |

3) | $\frac{2905}{1000}$ | $\frac{592}{100}$ | $\frac{9025}{1000}$ | $\frac{5209}{1000}$ |

28b

1) On Earth, the oldest rocks on the land are 3962 million years old. The oldest rocks beneath the sea are only about one-twentieth as old. About how old are the oldest rocks beneath the sea?

2) The Sahara desert is the largest in the world. It is 8 400 000 square kilometres in area. Only one fifth of the area is sand. The rest is stone and pebbles. How much of the area is stone and pebbles?

3) A 24-screen cinema complex in Brussels has 7000 seats. A cinema in New York City has about $\frac{9}{10}$ as many seats as the Brussels complex. How many seats has the cinema in New York City?

4) In a sponsored pogo-stick jump, Jimmy jumped 9·66 kilometres in $6\frac{1}{4}$ hours. After 3 hours he had jumped two-thirds of the distance. How many kilometres did he jump in the first 3 hours?

5) A new-born baby has 350 bones. An adult has only about three-fifths of this number. About how many bones has an adult?

6) There are about one million animal species alive today. About six-sevenths of these are insects and only about one hundredth are mammals. How many species are insects and how many mammals?

28c A

Believe it or not!

1 In 1999 an American team made the world's largest flag. It measured 77·724 metres by 153·924 metres. About how many of your classrooms could you fit on this flag?

2 When he was 22 years old Robert Wadlow was 2·72 metres tall. How many centimetres short of 3 metres is this? How tall was he in feet and inches?

How tall are you?

3 When Pauline Musters was 19 years old she was only 0·61 metres tall. How much would she have to grow, in centimetres, to be as tall as you?

4 On 19 September 1992, five people peeled 482·2 kilograms of potatoes in 45 minutes. About how long did it take one person to peel 1000 grams of potatoes?

5 In 1965 a male goliath bird-eating spider was found in Venezuela. Its leg-span was 28 centimetres. How much bigger is this than your hand-span?

What other records do you know?

1 On average, Bogor (in Java) has only 41 days in each year when it does not thunder. What is an approximate ratio of non-thundery to thundery days each year?

2 At Nordkapp in Norway there are about 84 days of 'midnight sun', when the sun never sets. What is an approximate ratio of days when the sun never sets to the rest of the days in the year?

3 The Earth's total surface area is approximately 500 million square kilometres. The ratio of land to water is about 3 to 7. What area of the surface is land and how much of the surface is covered by water?

4 Forests and hot deserts cover about 65·6 million square kilometres of the Earth's surface in the ratio of 4 m^2 of forest to 3 m^2 of hot desert. About how many square kilometres of the Earth's surface is hot desert?

B

1 Of the Earth's total land area of approximately 150 million square kilometres, 37·5 million square kilometres are forest. What proportion of the land is forest?

2 Out of 375 000 plant species that grow on Earth, 2 in every 3 are flowering plants. How many flowering plants are there?

3 Sloths spend 3 in every 4 hours hanging upside down. How many hours will they spend upside down in a week?

4 The black mamba snake is found in Africa. Out of every 20 people that it bites, 19 die. If 150 people were bitten, how many do you estimate would die?

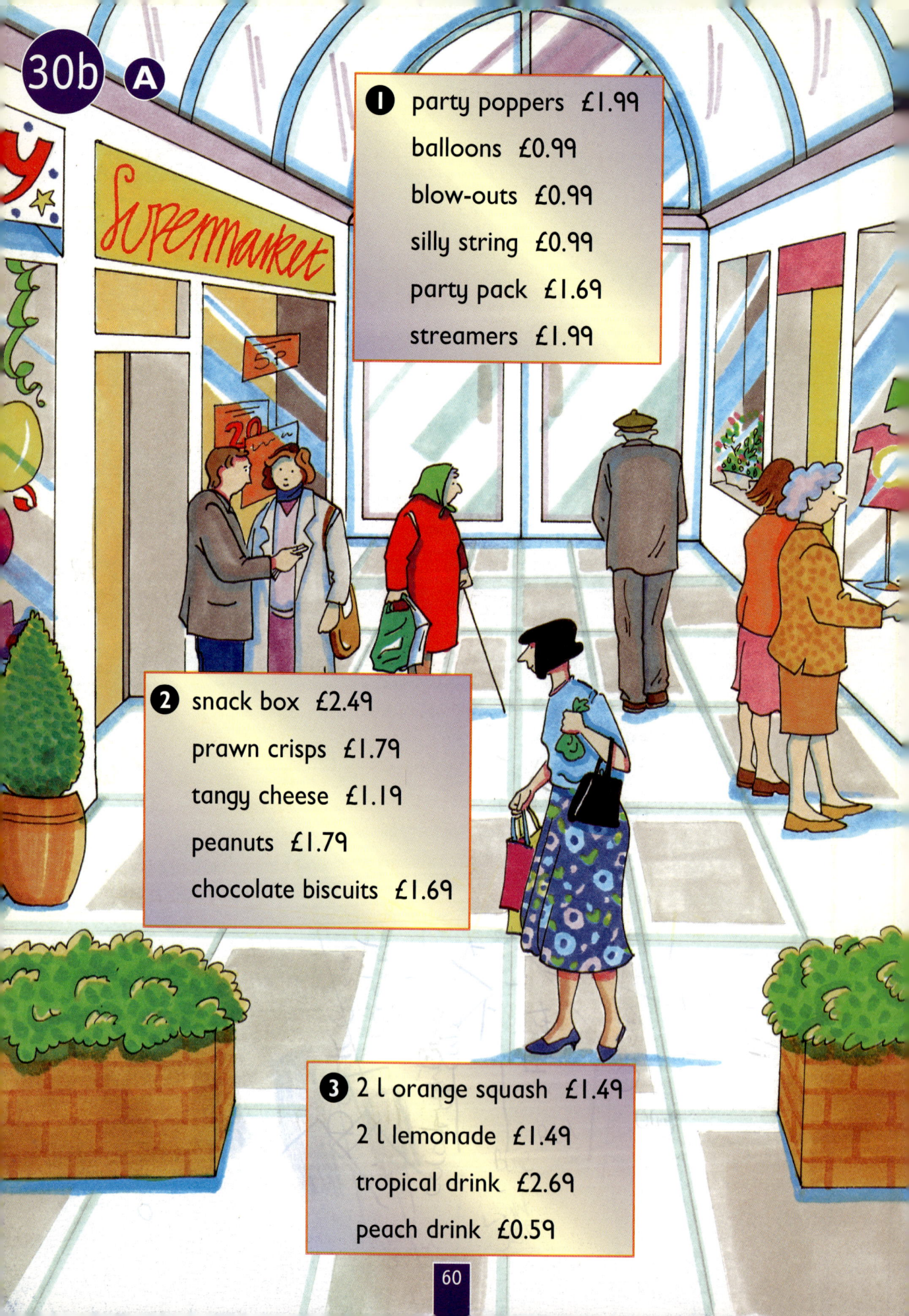

30b A

❶
party poppers £1.99
balloons £0.99
blow-outs £0.99
silly string £0.99
party pack £1.69
streamers £1.99

❷
snack box £2.49
prawn crisps £1.79
tangy cheese £1.19
peanuts £1.79
chocolate biscuits £1.69

❸ 2 l orange squash £1.49
2 l lemonade £1.49
tropical drink £2.69
peach drink £0.59

B

 C

① (24 + 57) ÷ (107 − 89)   ② (13 × 41) + (23 × 32)

③ (65 − 48) × (72 − 28)   ④ (157 − 82) ÷ (94 − 79)

1. There is a crowd of 3542 people at the Wonder Stadium. Tickets cost £3.30 each. How much money is collected?

2. Every season the Wonder Stadium orders 135 200 programmes. The printer packs the programmes into boxes of 130 programmes. How many boxes of programmes does the Stadium receive from the printer?

3. Programmes cost 85p each. At the Stadium concert on Saturday the total money from programme sales was £4370.70. How many programmes did they sell?

4. On the hot dog stall they took £686. Seventy-five per cent of the takings are profit. How much profit did they make?

5. Once a month a party of 211 school children and 18 adults go to the Stadium for sports practice. Coaches take no more than 54 people. How many coaches do they need to take them there?

31a

1 Number of cubes pulled out of a bag of ten after 100 goes

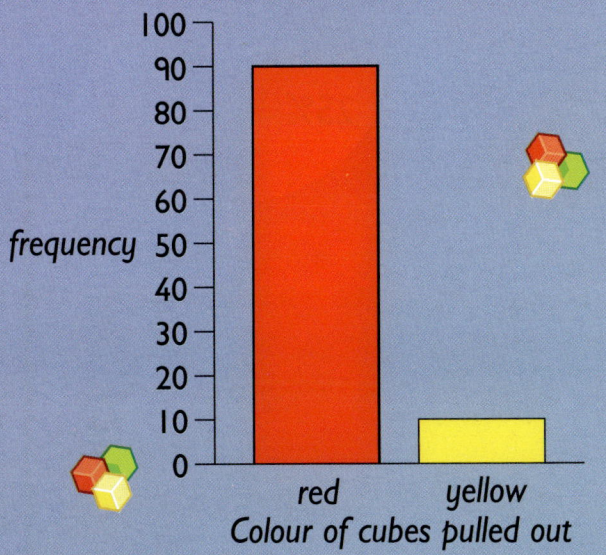

2 Number of cubes pulled out of a bag of ten after 100 goes

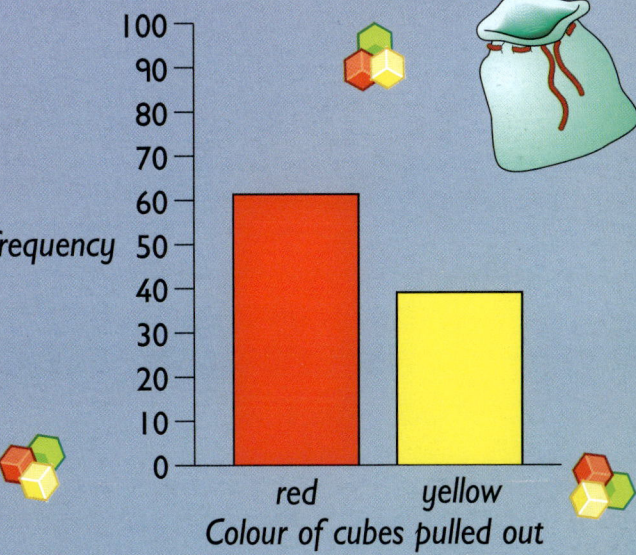

3 Number of cubes pulled out of a bag of ten after 50 goes

Colour of cube	Frequency
Red	9
Yellow	41

4 Number of cubes pulled out of a bag of ten after 100 goes

Colour of cube	Frequency
Red	48
Yellow	31
Green	21

5 Number of cubes pulled out of a bag of ten after 200 goes

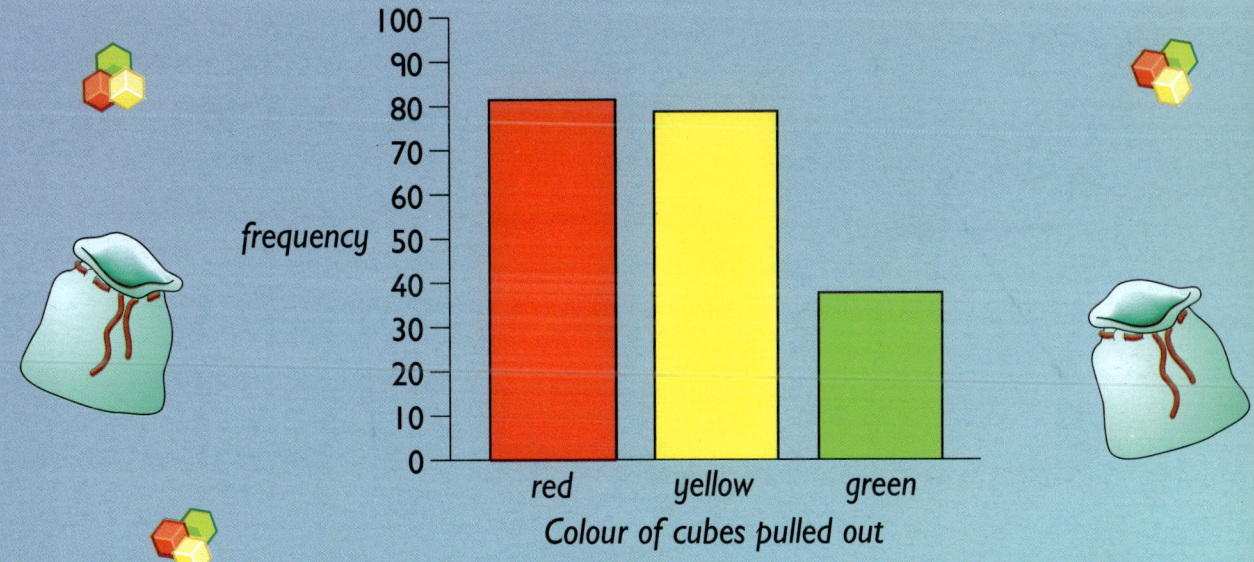

31b

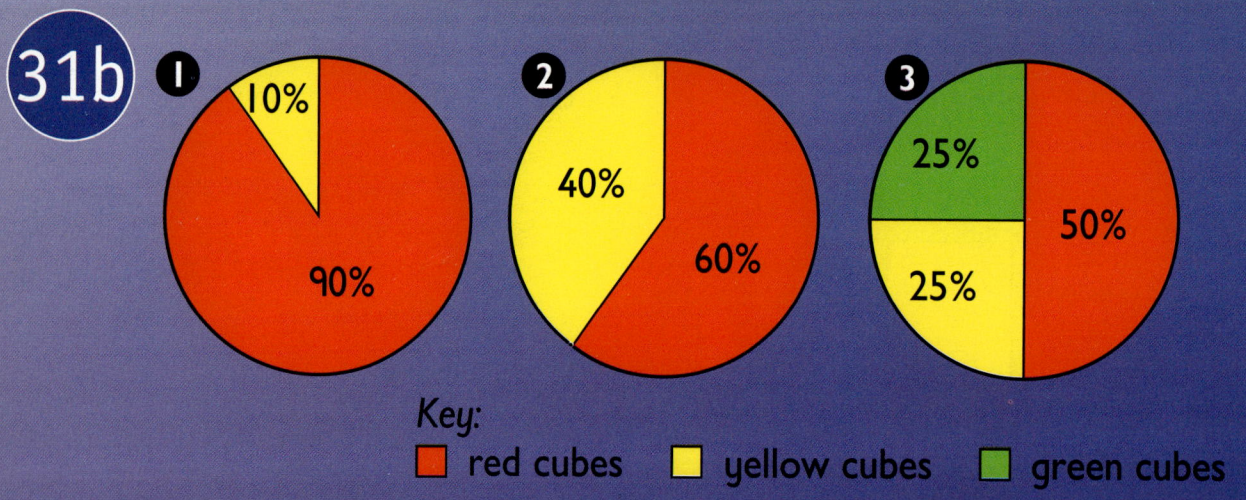

Key:
- red cubes
- yellow cubes
- green cubes

31c

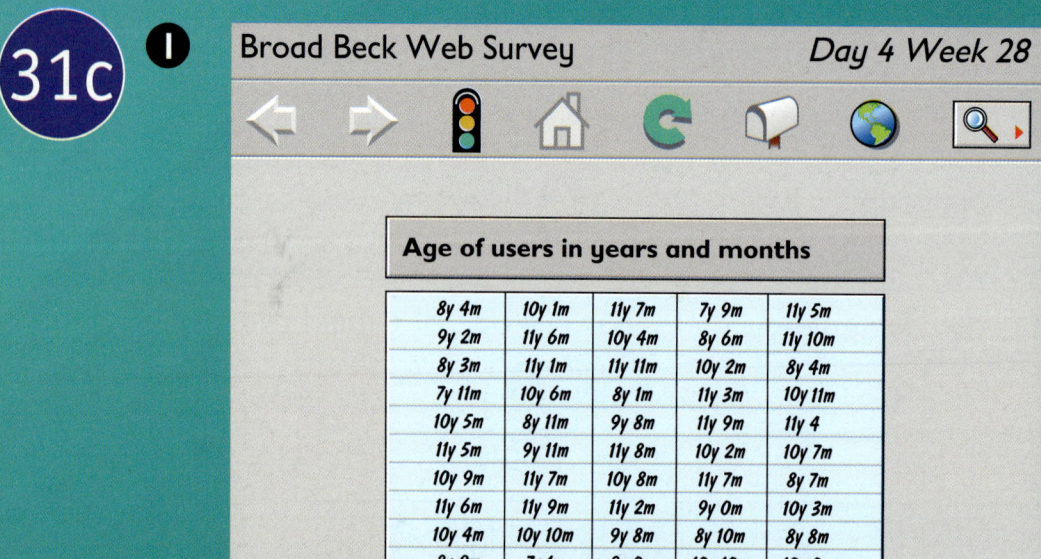

Broad Beck Web Survey — Day 4 Week 28

Age of users in years and months

8y 4m	10y 1m	11y 7m	7y 9m	11y 5m
9y 2m	11y 6m	10y 4m	8y 6m	11y 10m
8y 3m	11y 1m	11y 11m	10y 2m	8y 4m
7y 11m	10y 6m	8y 1m	11y 3m	10y 11m
10y 5m	8y 11m	9y 8m	11y 9m	11y 4
11y 5m	9y 11m	11y 8m	10y 2m	10y 7m
10y 9m	11y 7m	10y 8m	11y 7m	8y 7m
11y 6m	11y 9m	11y 2m	9y 0m	10y 3m
10y 4m	10y 10m	9y 8m	8y 10m	8y 8m
8y 9m	7y 1m	8y 0m	10y 10m	10y 0m

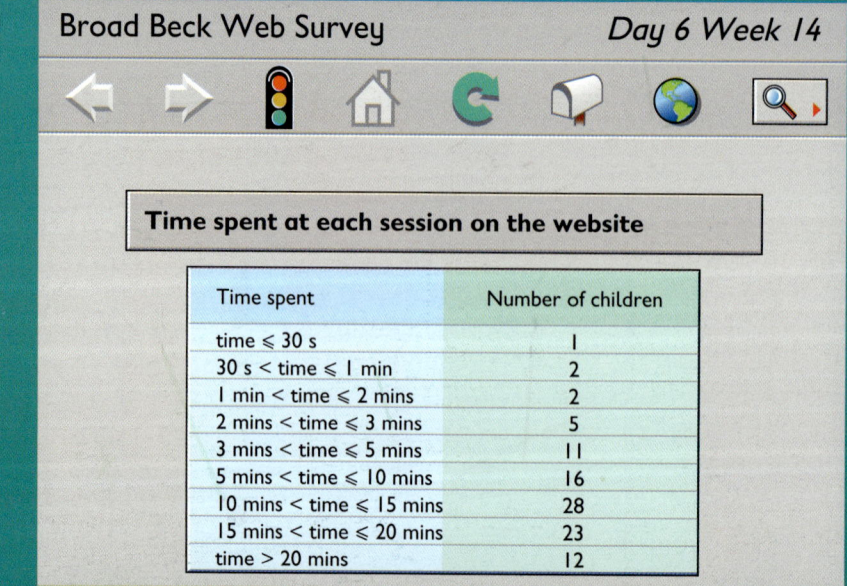

Broad Beck Web Survey — Day 6 Week 14

Time spent at each session on the website

Time spent	Number of children
time ≤ 30 s	1
30 s < time ≤ 1 min	2
1 min < time ≤ 2 mins	2
2 mins < time ≤ 3 mins	5
3 mins < time ≤ 5 mins	11
5 mins < time ≤ 10 mins	16
10 mins < time ≤ 15 mins	28
15 mins < time ≤ 20 mins	23
time > 20 mins	12

❸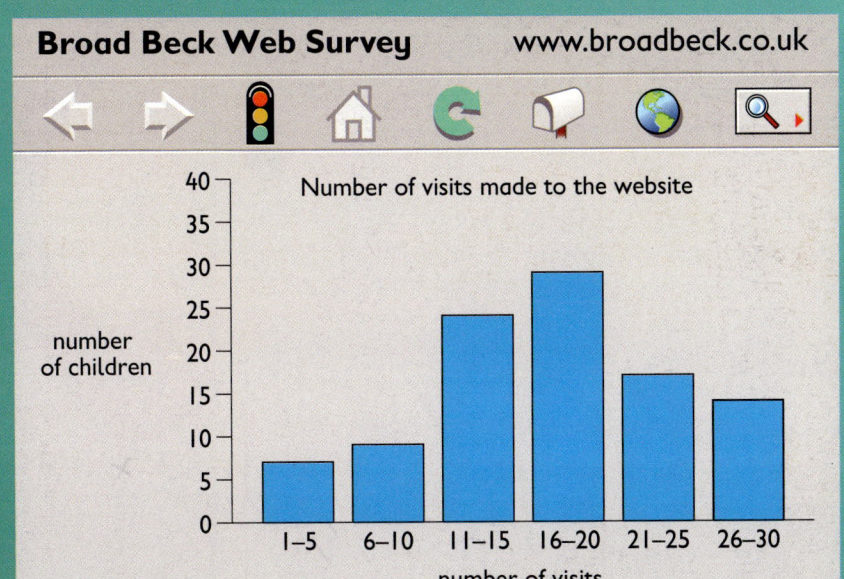

❹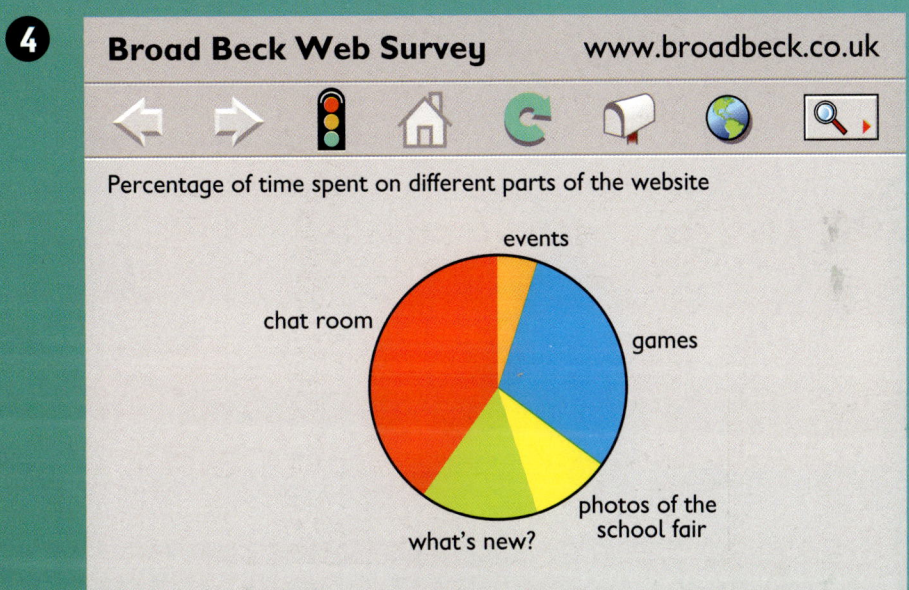

❺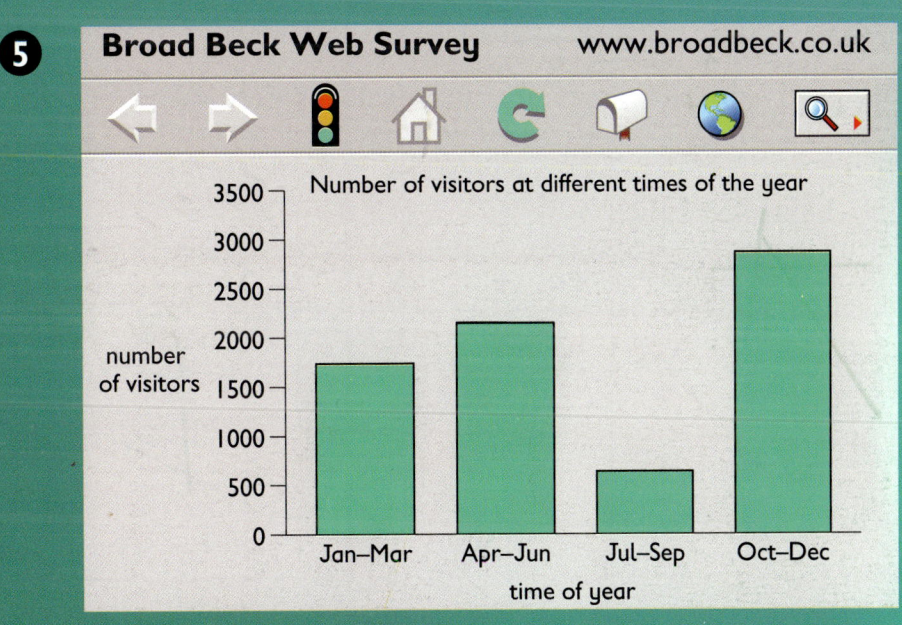

32a

A

1
2
3
4
5

B

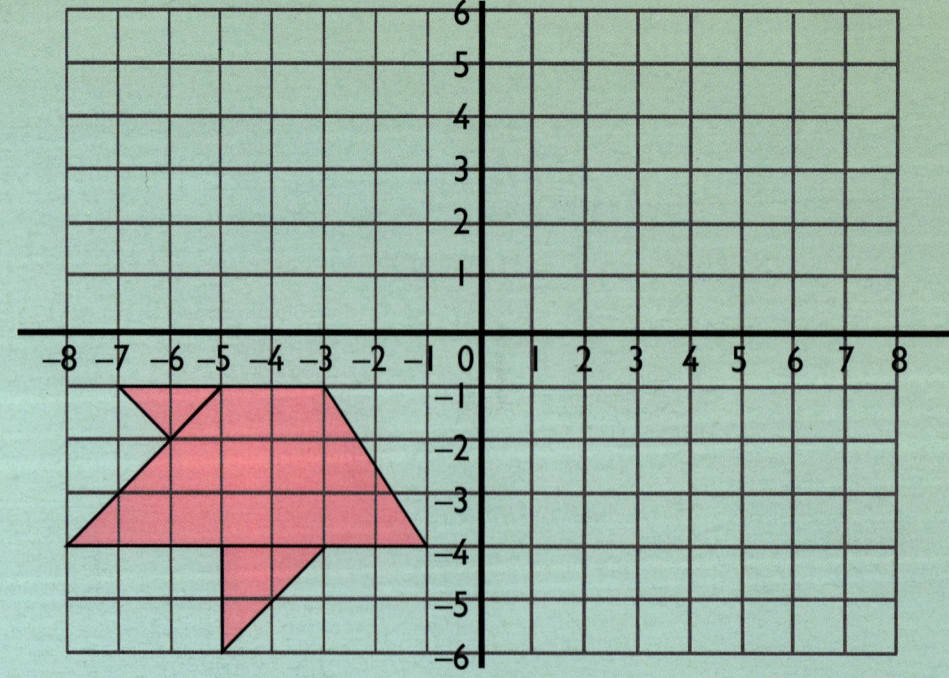

1. 4 squares right, 3 squares down
2. 5 squares up, 2 squares left
3. 2 squares left, 3 squares down
4. 4 squares up, 6 squares right
5. 3 squares down, 4 squares right

33a

A Flights between London and cities around the world

From	Departure day	Departure time	To
London	Monday	12:00 GMT	Athens, Greece
Athens, Greece	Monday	12:00 Local time	London
London	Monday	12:00 GMT	San Francisco, USA
San Francisco	Monday	12:00 Local time	London
London	Monday	13:00 GMT	Mexico City
Mexico City	Monday	13:00 Local time	London
London	Monday	22:30 GMT	Accra, Ghana
Accra, Ghana	Monday	22:30 Local time	London
London	Monday	11:00 GMT	Tokyo, Japan
Tokyo, Japan	Monday	11:00 Local time	London
London	Monday	22:00 GMT	Sydney, Australia
Sydney, Australia	Monday	22:00 Local time	London

B Flights between cities around the world

From	Departure day	Departure time	To
Sydney	Monday	21:00 Local time	San Francisco
San Francisco	Monday	21:00 Local time	Sydney
Auckland, New Zealand	Monday	13:00 Local time	Honolulu, Hawaii
Honolulu, Hawaii	Monday	13:00 Local time	Auckland, New Zealand

```
12:00    15:00    18:00    21:00    00:00     03:00    06:00    09:00    12:00
midday                              midnight                             midday
```

Arrival day	Arrival time		Flight time
Monday	18:00	Local time	4 hours
Monday	14:00	GMT	4 hours
Monday	14:00	Local time	10 hours
Tuesday		GMT	10 hours
Monday	17:30	Local time	10·5 hours
Tuesday		GMT	10·5 hours
Tuesday	05:00	Local time	6·5 hours
Tuesday		GMT	6·5 hours
Tuesday	07:30	Local time	11·5 hours
Monday		GMT	11·5 hours
Wednesday	08:00	Local time	24 hours
Tuesday		GMT	24 hours

Arrival day	Arrival time		Flight time
Monday	16:30	Local time	13·5 hours
Wednesday	04.30	Local time	13·5 hours
Sunday (previous day)	23:00	Local time	8 hours
Tuesday	19:00	Local time	8 hours

15:00 18:00 21:00 00:00 03:00 06:00 09:00 12:00
                    midnight   midday

Flight information	Ballooning companies			
	Fly High	**Up-in-the-Air**	**Clouds View**	**Heavens Aloft**
Days flights available	Daily	Daily	Sat/Sun	Daily
Flight times: Summer a.m. Summer p.m. Winter a.m. Winter p.m.	06:00 19:30 08:45 14:45	06:30 18:30 07:30 14:00	06:00 18:00 — —	05:45 18:45 09:15 14:15
Duration of flight	1·25 hrs	1·5 hrs	1 hr	1 hr
Speed of flight	24 km/h	9·5 miles/hr	12 miles/hr	16 km/h
Height of flight	400 m	600 feet	1000 feet	500 m
Distance of flight	35 km	15 miles	25 miles	16 km
Age limit	6 years	Under 14 with parent	8 years	8 years
Minimum height per person	1 m	3 feet	1·2 m	1·1 metres
Maximum passengers per flight	4	5	6	10
Cost per person: Weekday morning Weekday evening Weekends Children under 14	£135 £145 £150 £125	£130 £140 £145 £120	— — £135 £105	£115 £120 £125 £99

34a

1 There are 420 ml of juice in the glass. The bottle holds five and a quarter times as much.
How much juice does it hold?

2 A cask holds 825 cl of grape juice. A bottle holds 75 cl of grape juice. How many full bottles of grape juice can you get from the cask?

3 Pedro has a 7 litre barrel of olive oil. He fills 9 bottles with 75 cl each of olive oil. How much olive oil is left in his barrel?

4 The slush machine in Fred's Bar contains 4·5 litres of slush when full. A small slush drink is 330 ml, a medium slush is 500 ml, and a large slush is 700 ml. How much is left when Fred has sold 2 small, 1 medium and 3 large slushes?

5 The chemist makes up bottles of cough medicine in doses of 5 ml. She makes up one bottle for five days at 4 doses per day, one bottle for seven days at 5 doses per day, and one bottle for 14 days at 3 doses per day. How much medicine does she put in the three bottles?

34b

1 Kiwi fruit conditioner £2.40 per pint

2 Banana shampoo £22.50 per gallon

3 Coconut conditioner £3.60 per pint

4 Mango 2-in-1 shampoo and conditioner £29.25 per gallon

5 Turnip shampoo £16.65 per gallon

6 Pineapple conditioner £1.80 per pint

34c

A

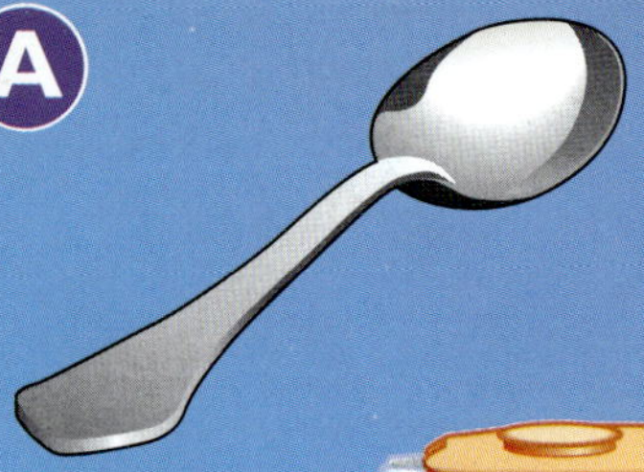
tea spoon

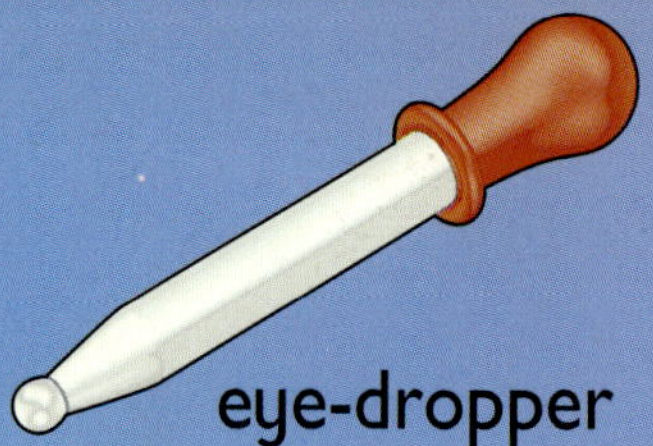
eye-dropper

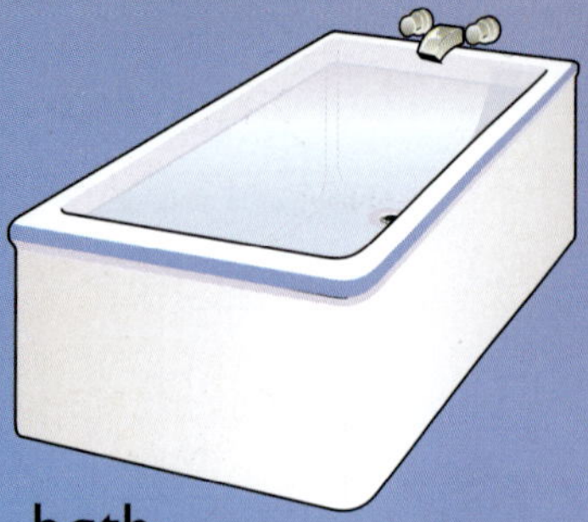
bath

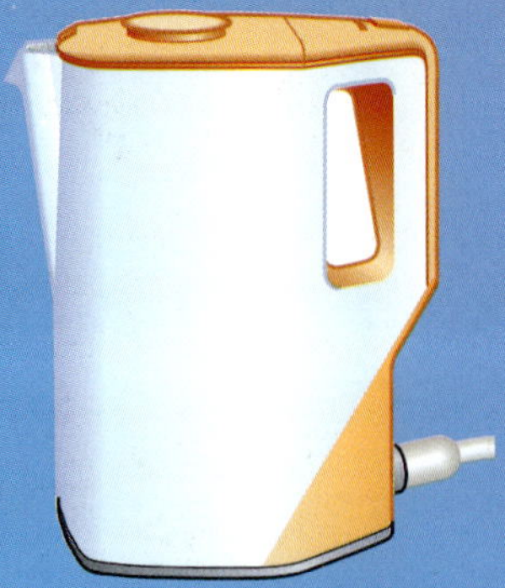
kettle

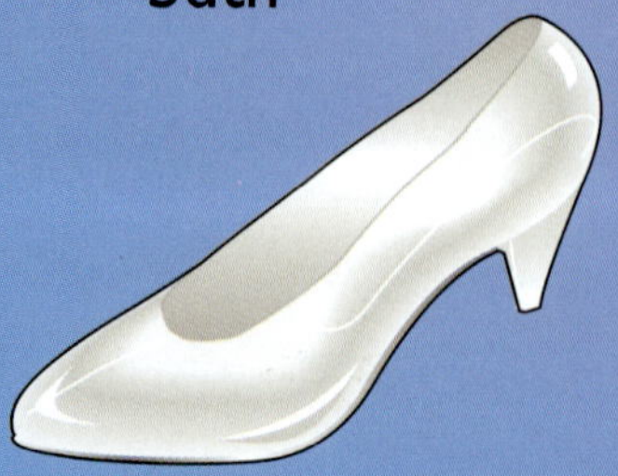
glass slipper

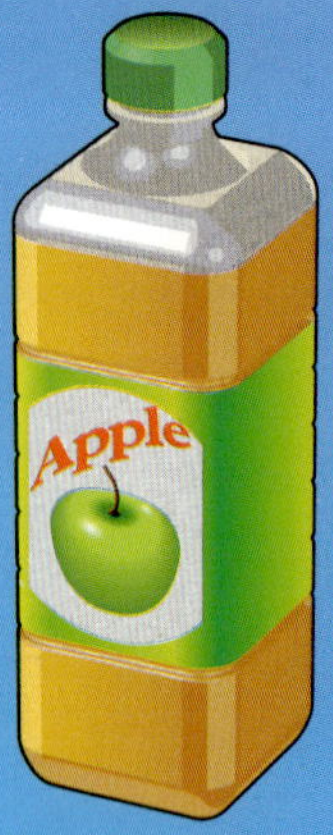
Apple
squash bottle

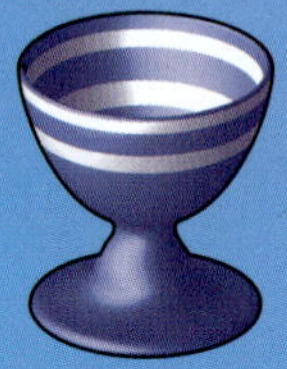
egg cup

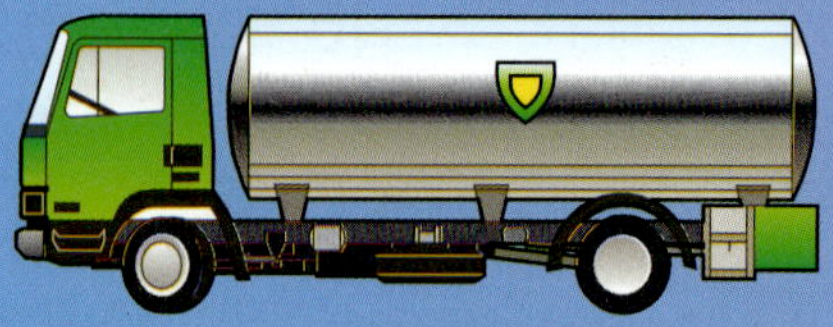
tanker

B

1
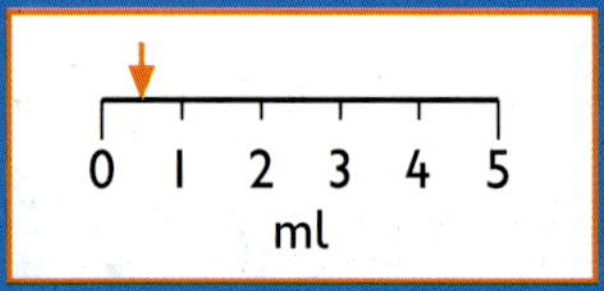
0 1 2 3 4 5
ml

2
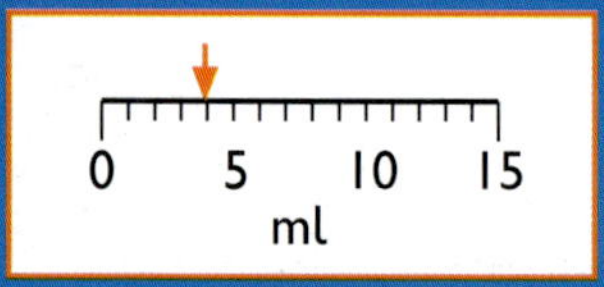
0 5 10 15
ml

3
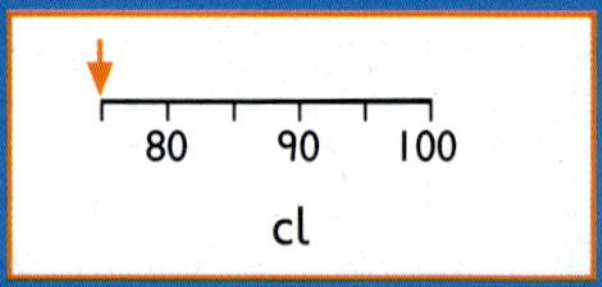
80 90 100
cl

4
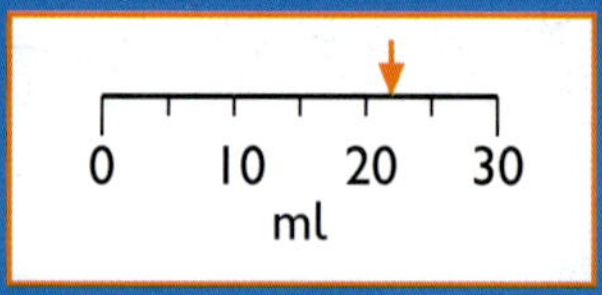
0 10 20 30
ml

5
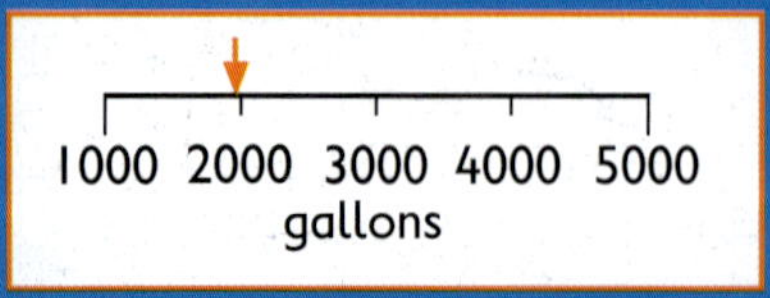
1000 2000 3000 4000 5000
gallons

6
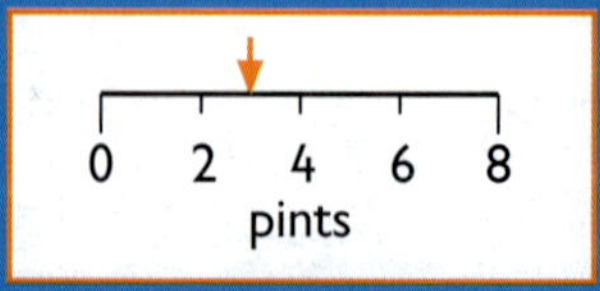
0 2 4 6 8
pints

7
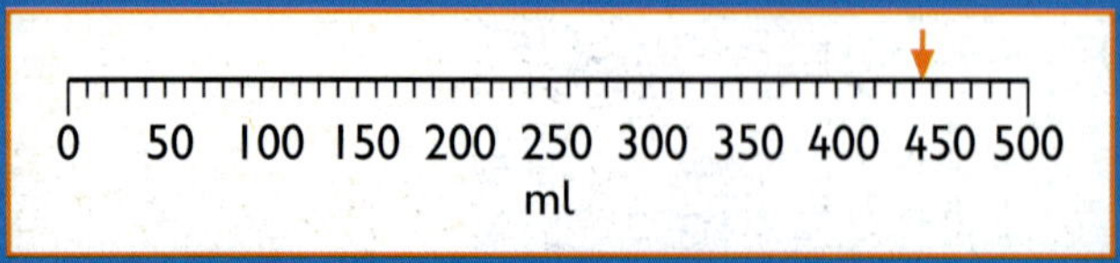
0 50 100 150 200 250 300 350 400 450 500
ml

8
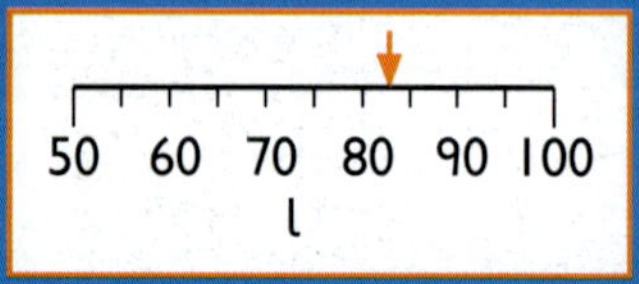
50 60 70 80 90 100
l

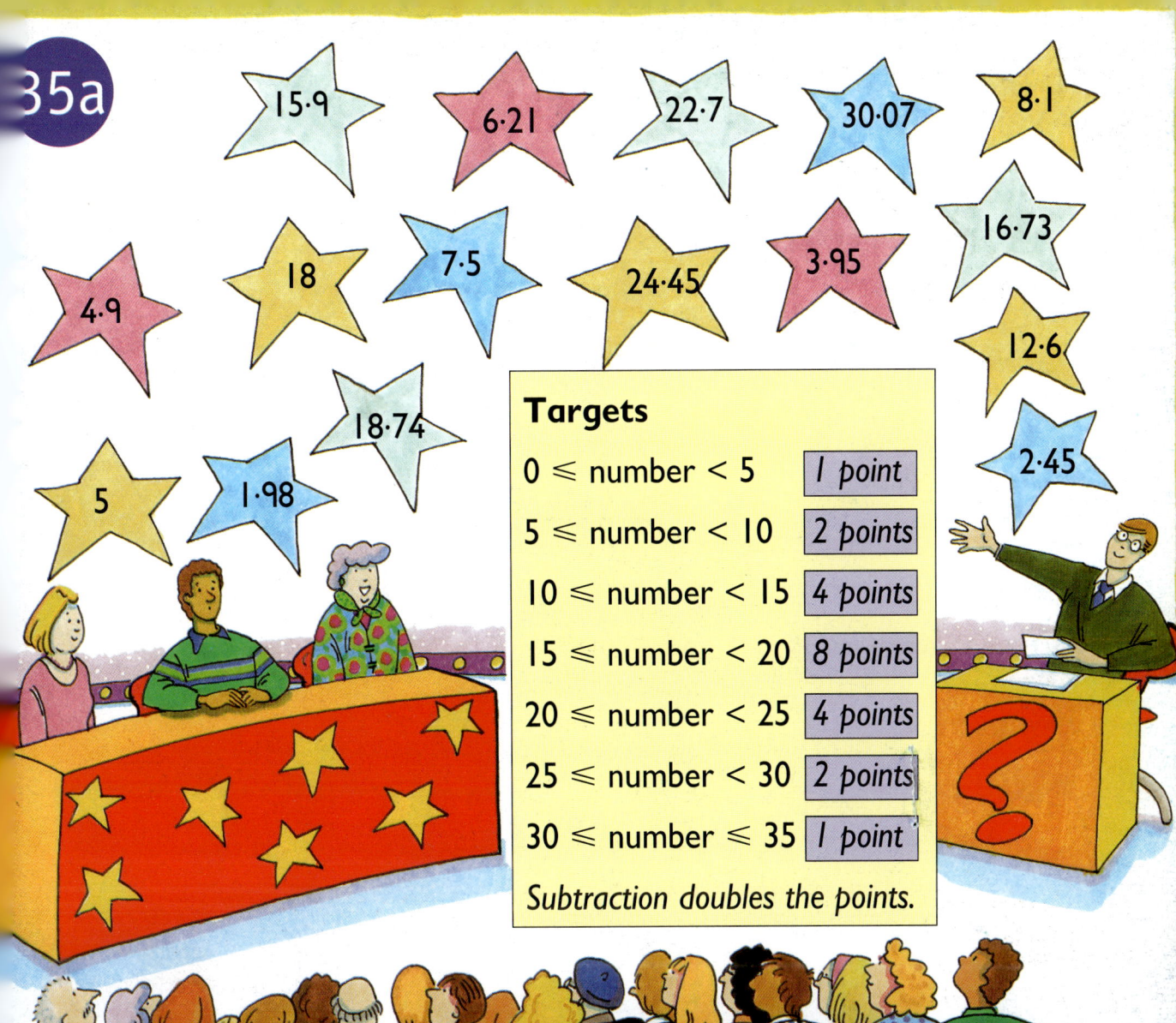

35c

1 Tufts pet show lasts 3 days. Last year 4786 people visited. This year 1289 people visited on day one and 1356 visited on day two. It costs £1.75 to get into the show. How many people have to visit on day three this year to beat the number of people visiting last year?

2 There were 523 rabbits and 284 guinea pigs entered for Tufts pet show this year. Rabbit hutches were set out in groups of 16 and guinea pig hutches in groups of 12. It cost £2.25 to enter a rabbit and £1.50 to enter a guinea pig. How many groups of hutches needed to be set out for the rabbits?

3 There were 1685 people who entered pets in the Tufts show. They were all given a questionnaire to fill in. Eighty per cent of the people given a questionnaire returned it. Sixty per cent of the people returning the questionnaire indicated that they had two or more pets. How many people were given a questionnaire?